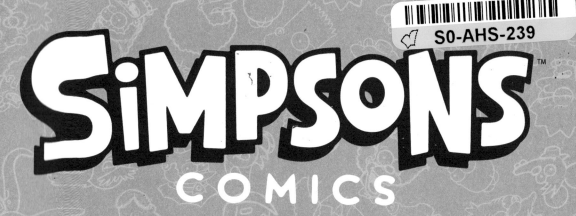

SiMPSONS
COMICS

COLOSSAL
COMPENDIUM
VOLUME THREE

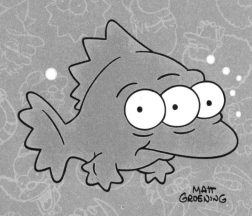

MATT GROENING

HARPER

NEW YORK • LONDON • TORONTO • SYDNEY

SIMPSONS COMICS COLOSSAL COMPENDIUM
VOLUME THREE

Materials previously published in
Bart Simpson #48, Bart Simpson's Pal Milhouse #1, Li'l Homer #1, Maggie #1,
The Malevolent Mr. Burns #1, Professor Frink Fantastic Science Fictions #1,
Ralph Wiggum Comics #1, Simpsons Comics #155, 162, 180, 186,
Simpsons Super Spectacular #9

FIRST EDITION
ISBN 978-0-06-236059-5
15 16 17 18 19 TC 10 9 8 7 6 5 4 3 2 1

Publisher: Matt Groening
Creative Director: Nathan Kane
Managing Editor: Terry Delegeane
Director of Operations: Robert Zaugh
Art Director: Jason Ho
Art Director Special Projects: Serban Cristescu
Assistant Art Director: Mike Rote
Production Manager: Christopher Ungar
Assistant Editor: Karen Bates
Production: Art Villanueva
Administration: Ruth Waytz, Pete Benson
Legal Guardian: Susan A. Grode

Printed by TC Transcontinental, Beauceville, QC, Canada. 05/15/2015

SIDESHOW SLOB
WELCOME BACK TO EVERYONE'S FAVORITE GAME SHOW, "FACE OR GUT?"
YOU'VE GOT FIVE SECONDS TO DECIDE!
MATT GROENING

IAN BOOTHBY SCRIPT | JOHN DELANEY PENCILS | ANDREW PEPOY INKS | ART VILLANUEVA COLORS | KAREN BATES LETTERS | BILL MORRISON EDITOR

PICK THE FACE! NO, THE GUT!
UM...
I'LL TAKE WHAT'S IN THAT BOX!
THIS IS **MY** BOX! YOU CAN'T HAVE IT!
AAAAAH!
WAIT A MINUTE! I RECOGNIZE THAT VOICE!
SIDESHOW BOB!!
AH, BART SIMPSON, MY OLD NEMESIS! YES, BEHOLD HOW FAR YOUR FORMER FOE HAS FALLEN!
SPARE CHANGE FOR A SCONE AND A HOT CUP OF DARJEELING TEA?
YOU NEED TO GET SOME SELF-RESPECT!
HEY, ARE YOU GONNA FINISH THAT BEER?

BEFORE I RUN AWAY, I GOTTA KNOW...WHAT HAPPENED TO YOU?
"WELL, AFTER MY LAST ATTEMPT TO MURDER YOU FAILED..."
"...I HAD A BIT OF TIME TO THINK."
"I REALIZED THAT I'D SPENT SO MUCH TIME TRYING TO GET REVENGE ON YOU THAT I'D LET MY OWN LIFE SLIP AWAY."
WELCOME TO POINTY ROCK CANYON!
"I TRIED A SERIES OF JOBS, BUT WITHOUT MY HATRED OF YOU SPURRING ME ON, I HAD LOST ALL AMBITION."
"I COULDN'T EVEN HOLD THE MOST MENIAL POSITION."
"I EVEN TURNED MYSELF IN AND WENT BACK TO PRISON, BUT I JUST DEPRESSED THE OTHER PRISONERS...SO THEY RELEASED ME."
NOW THE ***GUTTER*** IS MY HOME.
RATS ARE MY ONLY FRIENDS. ISN'T THAT RIGHT, WILBUR?
AAAAH!
OH, WHY DO YOU FIND MY EYES SO DELICIOUS?!
NICE CATCHING UP, BOB! SMELL YA LATER!

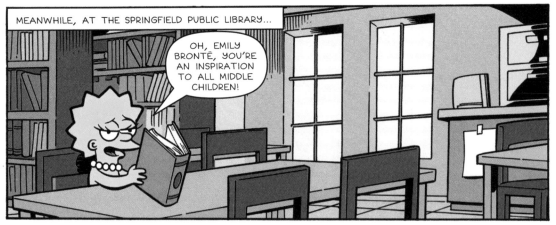

MEANWHILE, AT THE SPRINGFIELD PUBLIC LIBRARY...

OH, EMILY BRONTË, YOU'RE AN INSPIRATION TO ALL MIDDLE CHILDREN!

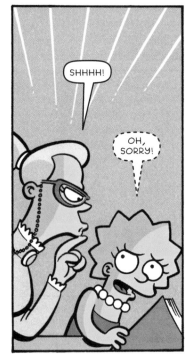

SHHHH!

OH, SORRY!

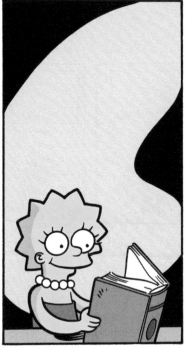

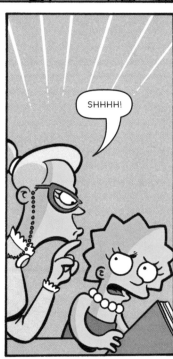

SHHHH!

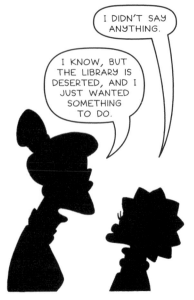

I DIDN'T SAY ANYTHING.

I KNOW, BUT THE LIBRARY IS DESERTED, AND I JUST WANTED SOMETHING TO DO.

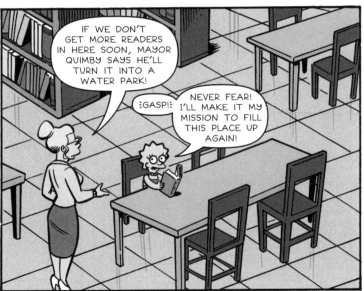

IF WE DON'T GET MORE READERS IN HERE SOON, MAYOR QUIMBY SAYS HE'LL TURN IT INTO A WATER PARK!

¡GASP!¡

NEVER FEAR! I'LL MAKE IT MY MISSION TO FILL THIS PLACE UP AGAIN!

SO, SIDESHOW BOB IS LIVING IN A CARDBOARD BOX? THIS I GOTTA SEE!
THEN CAST YOUR FOUR PEEPERS DOWN THIS ALLEY!
I'M A MAN OF MEANS BY NO MEANS!
KING OF THE ROOOOOAD!
CHESTER J. LAMPWICK! WHAT ARE YOU DOING HERE? YOU'RE NOT A BUM ANYMORE! YOU GOT RICH WHEN YOU WON THE RIGHTS TO ITCHY AND SCRATCHY!
THAT'S TRUE! THIS IS A GUCCI BINDLE SACK FILLED WITH FABERGÉ EGGS!
BUT EVERY ONCE IN A WHILE I MISS THE LIFE OF A BUM AND COME BACK TO MY OLD ALLEY!
THAT'S HOW I MET BOB HERE, A FEW DAYS AGO!
BUT HE'S AN ATTEMPTED MURDERER!
NOBODY'S PERFECT.
LOOK AT ME...I ONLY FLOSS ONCE A WEEK!

NOW WHAT WAS THAT THING YOU SAID YOU WANTED TO DO, BOB? RIDE THE RAILS, HOBO STYLE?
HOW I WISH WE COULD, OLD FRIEND, BUT THE RAILROAD STOPPED RUNNING THROUGH SPRINGFIELD YEARS AGO!
GIMME A SECOND!
HELLO? GET ME YOUR BOSS! NO, WAIT, GET ME YOUR BOSS'S BOSS!
I JUST BOUGHT THE RAILROAD. THEY'LL BE SENDING A TRAIN THROUGH TOWN IN TEN MINUTES!
AND SO...
ARE YOU SURE YOU DON'T WANT TO COME? THERE'LL BE SPITTING AND FOOT DANGLING!
SORRY, MY MOM DOESN'T WANT ME SPENDING TIME WITH HOBOS!
THAT SIDESHOW BOB IS UP TO SOMETHING!
COME BACK! I'VE BEEN WAITING YEARS FOR THAT TRAIN!

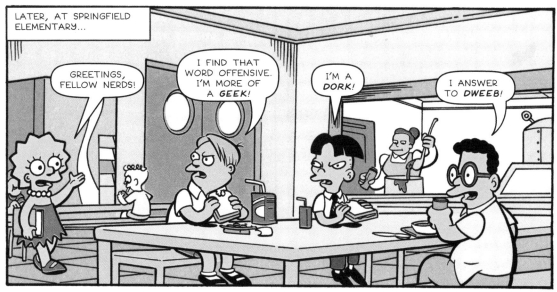

LATER, AT SPRINGFIELD ELEMENTARY...

GREETINGS, FELLOW NERDS!

I FIND THAT WORD OFFENSIVE. I'M MORE OF A *GEEK*!

I'M A *DORK*!

I ANSWER TO *DWEEB*!

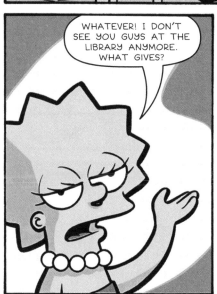

WHATEVER! I DON'T SEE YOU GUYS AT THE LIBRARY ANYMORE. WHAT GIVES?

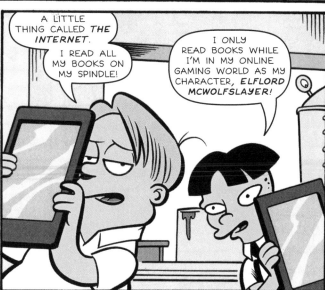

A LITTLE THING CALLED *THE INTERNET*. I READ ALL MY BOOKS ON MY SPINDLE!

I ONLY READ BOOKS WHILE I'M IN MY ONLINE GAMING WORLD AS MY CHARACTER, *ELFLORD MCWOLFSLAYER*!

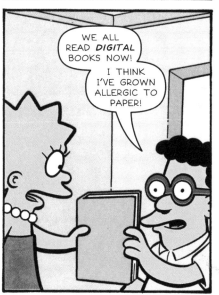

WE ALL READ *DIGITAL* BOOKS NOW! I THINK I'VE GROWN ALLERGIC TO PAPER!

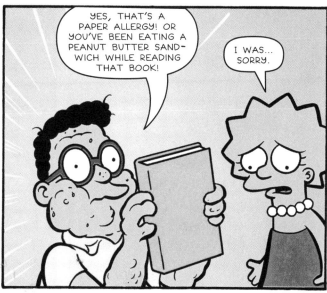

YES, THAT'S A PAPER ALLERGY! OR YOU'VE BEEN EATING A PEANUT BUTTER SAND- WICH WHILE READING THAT BOOK!

I WAS... SORRY.

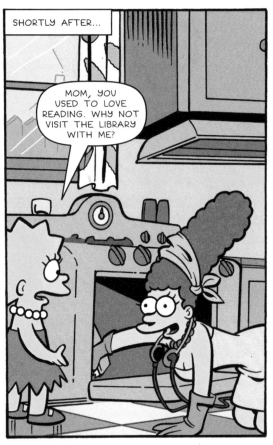

SHORTLY AFTER...

MOM, YOU USED TO LOVE READING. WHY NOT VISIT THE LIBRARY WITH ME?

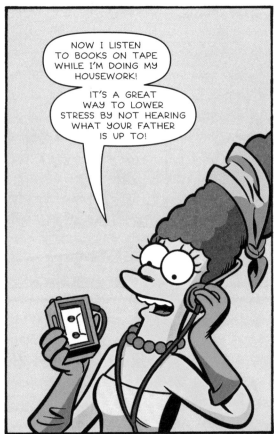

NOW I LISTEN TO BOOKS ON TAPE WHILE I'M DOING MY HOUSEWORK!

IT'S A GREAT WAY TO LOWER STRESS BY NOT HEARING WHAT YOUR FATHER IS UP TO!

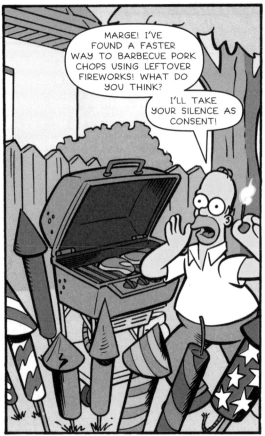

MARGE! I'VE FOUND A FASTER WAY TO BARBECUE PORK CHOPS USING LEFTOVER FIREWORKS! WHAT DO YOU THINK?

I'LL TAKE YOUR SILENCE AS CONSENT!

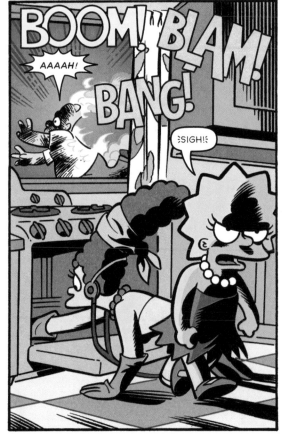

BOOM! BLAM!

AAAAH!

BANG!

:SIGH!:

THIS JUST IN: CHESTER J. LAMPWICK IS *DEAD!*
WHAT?
WHAT?!?!
YAAAAAH!
SHOVE!
TRAGEDY STRUCK TODAY WHEN A TRAIN MR. LAMPWICK WAS RIDING PLUNGED OFF THE AS YET *UNCOMPLETED* BLEEDING GUMS MURPHY MEMORIAL BRIDGE.
WE SPOKE WITH HIS BEST FRIEND.
HE DIED AS HE LIVED. SMELLY AND DRUNK.
HE WILL BE MISSED.
THIS JUST IN: IT APPEARS LAMPWICK'S WILL STATES THAT HIS VAST FORTUNE GOES TO...
...*SIDESHOW BOB!*
HIM?!!!
ME?

YOU KNOW WHAT TAKES MY MIND OFF **MY** TROUBLES?
VISITING THE LIBRARY!
REALLY?
EH...IT WAS WORTH A SHOT! I'M GOING TO GO TRY CONVINCING MILHOUSE!
WELL, NOW THAT I'M FANTASTICALLY WEALTHY, LET ME JUST SAY THIS...
...BART SIMPSON WILL **GET** WHAT'S COMING TO HIM!

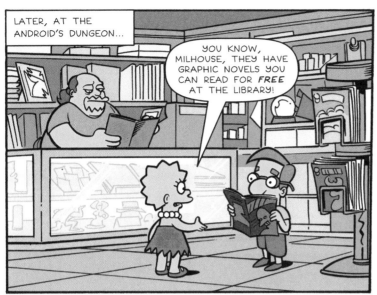

LATER, AT THE ANDROID'S DUNGEON...

YOU KNOW, MILHOUSE, THEY HAVE GRAPHIC NOVELS YOU CAN READ FOR *FREE* AT THE LIBRARY!

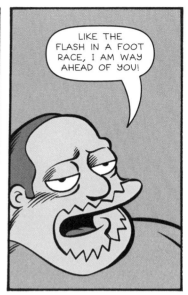

LIKE THE FLASH IN A FOOT RACE, I AM WAY AHEAD OF YOU!

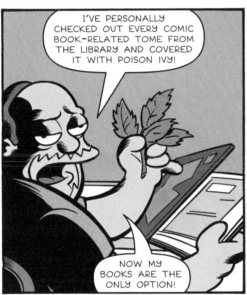

I'VE PERSONALLY CHECKED OUT EVERY COMIC BOOK-RELATED TOME FROM THE LIBRARY AND COVERED IT WITH POISON IVY!

NOW MY BOOKS ARE THE ONLY OPTION!

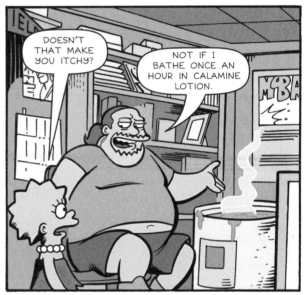

DOESN'T THAT MAKE YOU ITCHY?

NOT IF I BATHE ONCE AN HOUR IN CALAMINE LOTION.

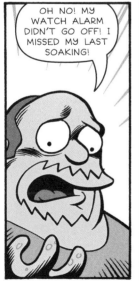

OH NO! MY WATCH ALARM DIDN'T GO OFF! I MISSED MY LAST SOAKING!

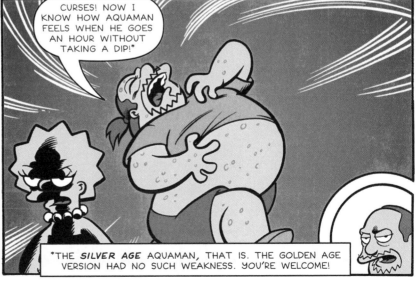

CURSES! NOW I KNOW HOW AQUAMAN FEELS WHEN HE GOES AN HOUR WITHOUT TAKING A DIP!*

*THE *SILVER AGE* AQUAMAN, THAT IS. THE GOLDEN AGE VERSION HAD NO SUCH WEAKNESS. YOU'RE WELCOME!

A FEW WEEKS LATER...
WE'RE CATCHING UP WITH FORMER PSYCHOPATH AND CURRENT ECCENTRIC MILLIONAIRE, SIDESHOW BOB!
HELLO, KENT! AS I PROMISED BEFORE, BART SIMPSON WILL NOW GET WHAT'S COMING TO HIM!
SEE! I TOLD YOU THAT'S WHAT HE SAID!
FINE! BUT THIS HAPPENS SO OFTEN YOU'RE LIKE THE BOY WHO CRIED WOLFMAN!
BART SIMPSON, I GIVE YOU...
...BARTLAND!
AN AMUSEMENT PARK DEDICATED TO THE SCAMP I ONCE TRIED TO KILL! I'M HAVING A SPECIAL PRIVATE PREVIEW FOR YOUNG BART TOMORROW THAT I HOPE HE WILL ATTEND!
BARTLAN
I AM SO SORRY, BART.
CAN YOU FORGIVE ME?
NO!
THE TV CAN'T HEAR YOU NO MATTER HOW LOUD YOU YELL, BOY! BELIEVE ME, I'VE TRIED!

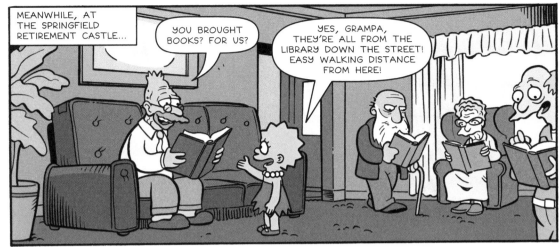

MEANWHILE, AT THE SPRINGFIELD RETIREMENT CASTLE...

YOU BROUGHT BOOKS? FOR US?

YES, GRAMPA, THEY'RE ALL FROM THE LIBRARY DOWN THE STREET! EASY WALKING DISTANCE FROM HERE!

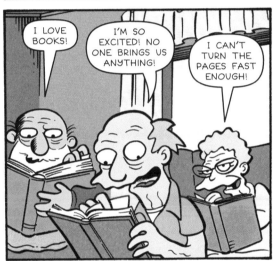

I LOVE BOOKS!

I'M SO EXCITED! NO ONE BRINGS US ANYTHING!

I CAN'T TURN THE PAGES FAST ENOUGH!

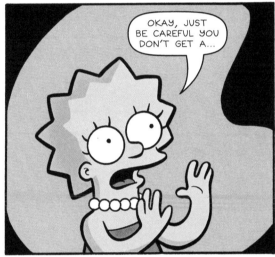

OKAY, JUST BE CAREFUL YOU DON'T GET A...

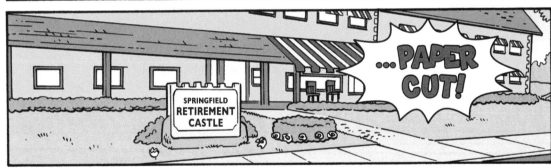

SPRINGFIELD RETIREMENT CASTLE

...PAPER CUT!

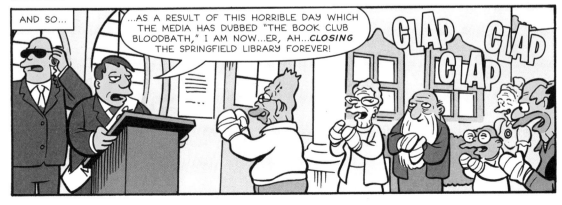

AND SO...

...AS A RESULT OF THIS HORRIBLE DAY WHICH THE MEDIA HAS DUBBED "THE BOOK CLUB BLOODBATH," I AM NOW...ER, AH...*CLOSING* THE SPRINGFIELD LIBRARY FOREVER!

CLAP CLAP CLAP

HEY, LISA! SORRY TO HEAR THEY CLOSED THE AQUARIUM!
IT WAS THE LIBRARY.
WHATEVER... LOOK, WOULD YOU COME TO BARTLAND WITH ME?
WHY ARE YOU EVEN GOING?
MEDIA PRESSURE!
PLEASE DO IT OR WE'LL HAVE TO FILL THE TIME WITH A REAL NEWS STORY!
A QUICK WALK LATER...
DON'T WORRY, BART. THESE RIDES WERE BUILT USING THE FINEST LOCAL DAY LABORERS!
WAIT, WUZ THESE NUTS SUPPOSED TO GO ON THEM THERE BOLTS?
NUTZ
THE PARK IS ALL YOURS!
WELCOME, BART SIMPSON, TO YOUR *ULTIMATE DAY ON EARTH!*
MY *ULTIMATE* DAY? THAT DOESN'T SOUND TOO BAD.
"ULTIMATE" ACTUALLY JUST MEANS "*LAST*."

YOU KNOW, I FEEL BAD NOW FOR BEING SO SUSPICIOUS. THIS ROLLER COASTER IS PRETTY COOL!
DO YOU WANT TO GO FASTER?
NO, WE'RE GOOD!
FASTER IT IS!
AAAAAH!
THE MANAGEMENT REGRETS TO INFORM YOU THAT THIS RIDE HAS NOT YET BEEN COMPLETED.
PLEASE KEEP YOUR HANDS IN THE VEHICLE! PERHAPS CLASPED TOGETHER TO SAY YOUR PRAYERS BEFORE YOU DIE, BART SIMPSON!
WHOOOOOA!
I DON'T THINK THAT WAS AN ACCIDENT!
REALLY? WHAT TIPPED YOU OFF?
SIDESHOW BOB'S COTTON CANDY

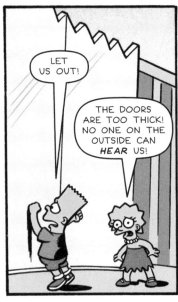

LET US OUT!

THE DOORS ARE TOO THICK! NO ONE ON THE OUTSIDE CAN *HEAR* US!

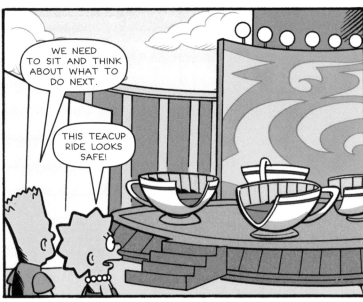

WE NEED TO SIT AND THINK ABOUT WHAT TO DO NEXT.

THIS TEACUP RIDE LOOKS SAFE!

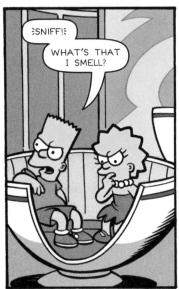

:SNIFF!:

WHAT'S THAT I SMELL?

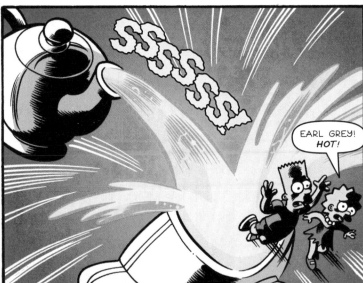

SSSSSS!

EARL GREY! *HOT!*

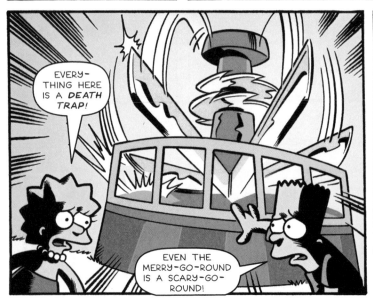

EVERY-THING HERE IS A *DEATH TRAP!*

EVEN THE MERRY-GO-ROUND IS A SCARY-GO-ROUND!

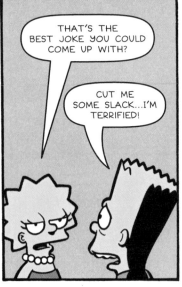

THAT'S THE BEST JOKE YOU COULD COME UP WITH?

CUT ME SOME SLACK...I'M TERRIFIED!

YAAAAH!
SMASH!
BART! I'VE GOT AN IDEA! MEET ME AT THE HOT DOG STAND!
I'VE WRITTEN "HELP" IN MUSTARD ON ALL THESE DOGS! WE'VE GOT TO GET THEM OVER THE WALL!
THEN JUMP IN! THE OTHER BUMPER CARS ARE TRYING TO RUN ME OVER!
TOSS!
SECONDS LATER...
SMASH!
YOU GOT OUR MESSAGE!
WHAT MESSAGE? WE JUST WANTED MORE OF THOSE DELICIOUS HOT DOGS!

HALL OF MIRR
AND LOOK WHO I FOUND TIED UP IN THE HOUSE OF MIRRORS!
CHESTER J. LAMPWICK!
HOW DID YOU FIND ME IN THERE SO FAST?
HALLS OF MIRRORS ARE BUILT TO FOOL THE HUMAN EYE, NOT THE NOSE!
POINT TAKEN! I'LL UP MY SPONGE BATHS TO *TWICE* A MONTH!
YES, YES, LET'S JUST CUT TO THE CONFESSION! I FAKED LAMPWICK'S DEATH AFTER I MADE FRIENDS WITH HIM AND GOT HIM TO LEAVE ME EVERYTHING IN HIS WILL.
THEN I USED THE MONEY TO BUILD THIS ELABORATE DEATH TRAP FOR BART SIMPSON. AND I WOULD HAVE GOTTEN AWAY WITH IT TOO...
...EXCEPT FOR A SERIES OF FACTORS I DIDN'T CONSIDER!
LIKE US MEDDLING KIDS?
AMONG OTHERS... YES!
BUT... ***SURPRISE TWIST!*** I PLANNED FOR THIS AND RIGGED THE ENTIRE PARK TO ***EXPLODE*** WHEN I PUSH THIS BUTTON!
I'LL SEE YOU IN TARTARUS, BART!
IS THAT WHERE THEY MAKE THE SAUCE?
CLICK!

SORRY TO BOTHERS YA, MR. BOB, BUT WHAT DID YOU WANT ME TO ATTACH THIS HERE WIRE TO AGAIN?
THE DYNAMITE, YOU INCOMPETENT HICK!
HEY, IF YOU GOTS A COMPLAINT, TAKE IT UP WITH THE HEAD OF MY UNION!
OINK!
I'LL BE BACK, BART SIMPSON! YOU HAVEN'T SEEN THE LAST OF ME!
BONK!
WHY DID I EVEN BUILD THAT THING?

WELL, I'M GLAD YOU'RE SAFE AGAIN, BART, BUT I'M STILL DEPRESSED ABOUT THE LIBRARY CLOSING.
DID YOU SAY THEY CLOSED THE LIBRARY? BUT THAT WAS MY SECOND HOME, EVEN WHEN I DIDN'T HAVE A FIRST ONE!
DON'T YOU WORRY, LITTLE LADY, I'LL OPEN THAT PLACE BACK UP BY TOMORROW MORNING!
OH, THAT'S WONDERFUL!
THE NEXT MORNING...
♪ LA ♪ LA LA!
BACK OF THE LINE!
WHAT?
THERE'S A LINE TO GET IN?
IT'S OKAY. SHE'S WITH ME!

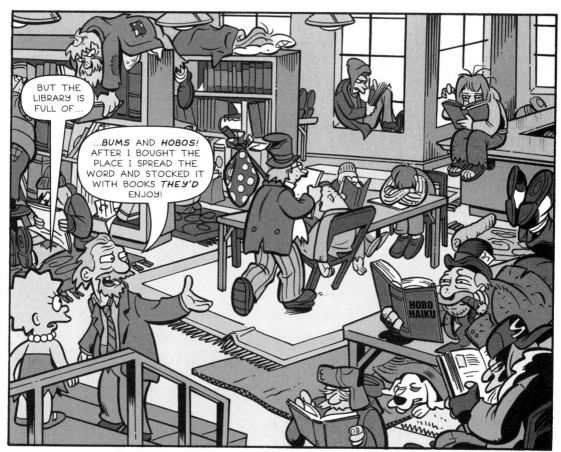

BUT THE LIBRARY IS FULL OF...

...*BUMS* AND *HOBOS*! AFTER I BOUGHT THE PLACE I SPREAD THE WORD AND STOCKED IT WITH BOOKS *THEY'D* ENJOY!

HOBO HAIKU

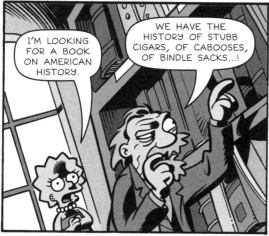

I'M LOOKING FOR A BOOK ON AMERICAN HISTORY.

WE HAVE THE HISTORY OF STUBB CIGARS, OF CABOOSES, OF BINDLE SACKS...!

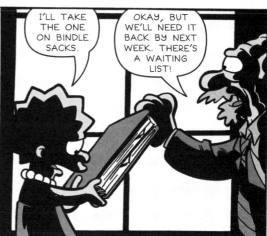

I'LL TAKE THE ONE ON BINDLE SACKS.

OKAY, BUT WE'LL NEED IT BACK BY NEXT WEEK. THERE'S A WAITING LIST!

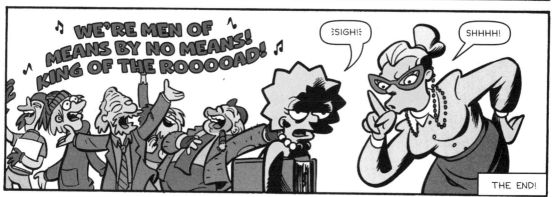

♪ WE'RE MEN OF MEANS BY NO MEANS! KING OF THE ROOOOAD! ♪

⸬SIGH!⸬

SHHHH!

THE END!

ANGRY DAD IN POPPIN' MAD
by BART SIMPSON
MMM...I THINK I'LL POP SOME FRESH POPCORN!
MATT GROENING
C'MON! C'MON! HURRY UP AND POP!
POUR!
BEEP!
ON
THIS OUGHTA SPEED THINGS UP. HEH-HEH!
ON
50° 100° 300° 500°
OH, NO!
POP CORN!
BULLETS
HIGHLY EXPLOSIVE! DO NOT HEAT!
ON
KA-BOOM!
WHY DO I SMELL BURNT BACON?
POP! POP!
POP CORN!
ON

TONY DIGEROLAMO
SCRIPT

JASON HO
PENCILS & INKS

ART VILLANUEVA
COLORS

KAREN BATES
LETTERS

BILL MORRISON
EDITOR

Little Monty Million$
ADVENTURE ON BIGFOOT MOUNTAIN!

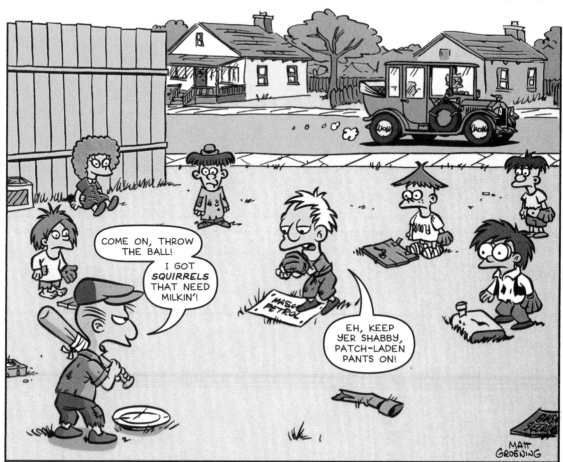

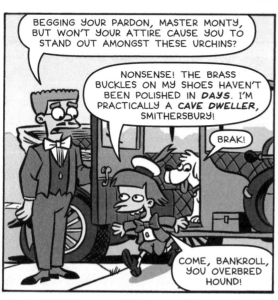

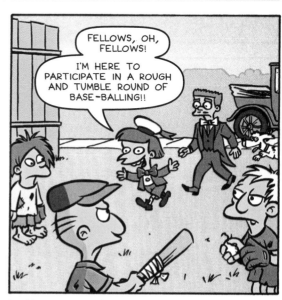

GAIL SIMONE
SCRIPT

MIKE KAZALEH
PENCILS & INKS

NATHAN HAMILL
COLORS

KAREN BATES
LETTERS

NATHAN KANE
EDITOR

WELL, WE ARE SHORT A MAN...
IS HE TALKIN' ENGLISH? 'CAUSE I DON'T UNDERSTAND WHAT THAT KID IS SAYIN'.
ALL RIGHT, YOU CAN PLAY RIGHT FIELD.
O FRABJOUS DAY!
I SHALL CAPTURE ALL THE BALLS IN MY ASSIGNED QUADRANT!
GOOD LUCK, NEW BOY. MY NAME'S SUE.
SUE! WELL, THAT'S WHAT MY FATHER DOES FOR SPORT!
I'M MONTY.
SOON...
I HAVE IT, CHUMS. DO NOT FEAR, FOR I HAVE INDEED CAUGHT THE...
AWWW, MONTY!
POOT!
THE OLD BURNS CHARM AND PHYSICAL PROWESS DO NOT SEEM TO BE WORKING WITH THIS LOT, SMITHERSBURY!
MASTER MONTY, WHY NOT SIMPLY LET YOUR FATHER BUY YOU SOME CLOSE FRIENDS AS USUAL?
NONSENSE! ON TO PLAN B!
OH, PLAYMATES! I'VE INVITED SOME OF MY NEIGHBORHOOD PALS TO PARTICIPATE IN OUR CONTEST. I HOPE YOU DON'T MIND!
WHAT NOW?

FRESH FROM THROWING THE GAME FOR MONEY IN THE 1919 WORLD SERIES, IT'S THE DISGRACED AND SURPRISINGLY AFFORDABLE CHICAGO WHITE SOX!
AND SO...
YAAH!
RAZZIN' FRAZZIN' WUZZA!
GLUG!
WHACK!
UMM...
AWW...
ULP!
HE WAS CROWDIN' THE PLATE!
Home Visitors
0 212

WELL, YOU ROONT THE GAME, NEW KID. THANKS.
BUT...BUT, WE WON!
AW, G'WAN HOME! YOU CRYBABIES PLAY WORSE THAN THE CARDINALS!
CONSIDERABLY WORSE!
I DON'T SUPPOSE I WILL EVER HAVE ANY REAL FRIENDS, SMITHERSBURY.
YOU HAVE ME, SIR.
OH, DO SHUT UP.
MONTY!
LISTEN, A FEW OF US ARE GOING CAMPING UP AT BIGFOOT MOUNTAIN...NOTHING FANCY, JUST TENTS AND STUFF. WHY DON'T YOU COME?
HRMMM...
OH, MY WORD, YES! SMITHERSBURY AND I GO CAMPING ALL THE TIME.
AND MONTY...TRY TO BE LIKE A NORMAL KID, OKAY?
OH, ABSOLUTELY. "NORMAL" IS MY MIDDLE NAME.
CHARLES MONTGOMERY BENEDICT NORMAL THELONIOUS RICHTHOFEN BURNS!
YOU'RE SILLY.
SMACK!
OH!
SMITHERSBURY! WHAT DO THE FOLLOWING WORDS MEAN?
"CAMPING," "TENT," AND ALSO "STUFF."

LATER, AT BIGFOOT MOUNTAIN...
WHATCHA LOOKIN' SAD FER, SUE? AIN'T YER WEINER BURNT ENOUGH?
OH, I JUST THOUGHT...
NEVER MIND.
SPUTTER! SPUT! SPUT! PUTT!
WHAT'S THAT WEIRD, GASSY SOUND?
WHY ARE YOU LOOKIN' AT ME?
IT AIN'T YOU. IT'S THAT!
HUZZAHS, MY BOSOM BUDDIES! I'M READY TO ROUGH IT, AS THE PIONEERS DID!
NOTICE HOW I HAVE BROUGHT THE AUTOGYRO WITH THE LEAST COMFORTABLE SEATS!
MB
DON'T MIND ME, MY LOWER CLASS COMPADRES!
JUST CONSIDER ME ONE OF THE GANG!
BRAK!
BUT SOON...
ER...IT SEEMS THAT MY MOUSSE DE FOIE GRAS KEEPS SLITHERING OFF THE STICK.
ISN'T THAT ALWAYS THE WAY, FELLOWS?

AND LATER...
...AND *THAT* WAS WHEN THE FATHER REALIZED THAT HIS MURDERED WIFE HAD FORGOTTEN TO FILE A JOINT RETURN LISTING HER MUNICIPAL EXPENDITURES!
YOU *STINK,* BURNS!
GOOD NIGHT AND *GOOD RIDDANCE!*
I DON'T GET IT. THAT ONE SCARES THE *PANTALOONS* OFF THE LADS AT THE JUNIOR SCHOONER CLUB!
MONTY...
GOOD NIGHT.
WILL YOU BE REQUIRING THE MATTRESS STUFFED WITH MONEY THIS EVENING, MASTER MONTY?
MB
NOT TONIGHT, SMITHERSBURY. I'M TOO BLUE.
SIGH!
$$$$
FRIG
ZZZZ
EEEK! MONTY! HELP!
EH?
SUSAN?
SOMETHING'S TAKEN SUE!
AND THE REST OF THE CHILDREN!
DON'T *CORRECT* ME, SMITHERSBURY!

OOOOOOWOO'NWOOO
WHAT IS THAT BEASTLY HOWL?!
DON'T YOU SEE, YOU OBSEQUIOUS LACKEY?
THE LEGENDS ARE TRUE!
THE SASQUATCH LIVES!
TO THE TRAIL, MAN!
BRAK!
BANKROLL, I SWEAR. I WILL HAVE YOU STUFFED, YOU INSIPID CUR!
YANK!
THESE TRACKS LEAD TO THAT HIDDEN CAVE!
BEWARE, SMITHERSBURY, THIS COULD GET STICKY!
BEHOLD...!

...THE LOST CITY OF THE KINGDOM OF THE LOST SASQUATCH PYRAMIDS OF BIGFOOT MOUNTAIN!
HMM...THAT TITLE'S A TRIFLE UNWIELDY, TO BE FRANK.

CAREFUL! AT ANY MOMENT ONE OF THESE BLOODTHIRSTY, SAVAGE, KILL-CRAZY BEASTS COULD TEAR US APART!
WE'LL BE PLUCKED AND EATEN LIKE A GOOSE ON BASTILLE DAY!
BRAK!

WELL, I SHOULD HAVE SEEN *THAT* COMING. PREDICTABLE, REALLY.

IT'S TIME TO SHOW OUR **METTLE**, SMITHERSBURY.
ONLY **ONE THING** TO DO AT A TIME LIKE THIS!
SACRIFICE THE PAWN TO SAVE THE KING!
SIR, I'M YOUR PERSONAL VALET!
SHOVE!
THAT'S SWEET OF YOU TO WORRY, BUT I HAVE SIMPLY ***OODLES*** OF REPLACEMENTS!
COURAGE, SMITHERSBURY!
BUT, SIR!
SIR! IT'S A ***FEMALE!***
AND IT'S TRYING TO ***WOO*** ME! ***SIIIIRR!***
MUCH LATER...
DEUCED THING... I ALMOST FEEL ***REGRET***, LEAVING THOSE PEOPLE DOWN THERE.
FETCH MY ADVENTURING UNDER-GARMENTS!
MB
SOON...
HERE WE ARE, BOYS!
THE ULTIMATE CONFRONTATION BETWEEN BEAST AND MAN!

LISTEN UP, YOU HIRSUTE SLACKADAISIES!
YOU ARE ALL BEING **EVICTED!**
THAT'S RIGHT, YOU FURRY FOPS! I JUST PURCHASED THIS **ENTIRE MOUNTAIN,** AND YOU ARE NO LONGER WELCOME!
?
DEED
ALL THESE PYRAMIDS WILL BE SMELTED INTO GOLDEN **ALL-WEATHER SIDING** FOR MY MANSION.
YOU WILL BE HUMANELY MOVED TO ZOOS AND SEWERS AND SO FORTH.
CHECK AND **MATE,** YOU SAVAGES!
THAT'S WHAT COMES OF TOYING WITH MY FRIENDS!
MONTY! **NO!**
THEY ONLY WANTED TO BE FRIENDS...THEY'VE DECIDED TO SHARE THEIR BOUNTY WITH US...WITH THE ENTIRE TOWN!
THEY'S **GOOD PEOPLE,** YA DANG FOOL!
THE BIG ONE THERE WAS TEACHIN' ME TO MAKE **EMPANADAS!**

WHILST I HAVE FOUND A MEANINGFUL RELATIONSHIP WITH DEBBIE, HERE!
BE HAPPY FOR ME, SIR!
SO YOU SEE, YOU HAVE TO GIVE THEM BACK THEIR HOME, MONTY.
HMM...NO, I THINK I'LL JUST ROLL THE DICE WITH THIS WHOLE MOUNTAIN OF GOLD THING. SEE WHERE THAT'S HEADING.
YOU KNOW, IT OCCURS TO ME THAT IF I ADD THIS TO THE MONEY IN MY PIGGY BANK, I COULD BUY SPRINGFIELD LOCK, STOCK, AND BARREL. WHAT TO DO WITH THIS WASTED ACREAGE, THOUGH...
BUT...
YOU KNOW, THIS WOULD BE AN EXCELLENT PLACE FOR A POWER PLANT!
MONTY!
YES. FINE.
YOU MAY HAVE MOUNTAINS OF GOLD. YOU MAY OWN THE TOWN.
YOU MAY EVEN OWN THE PEOPLE.
BUT YOU WILL NEVER HAVE FRIENDS, MONTGOMERY BURNS!
YES. AND IT TURNS OUT, I'M FINE WITH THAT!
START THE SMELTERS, BOYS!
HE'S A LITTLE STINKER, AIN'T HE? THE END.

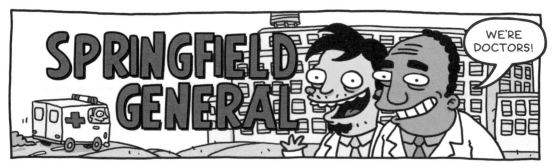

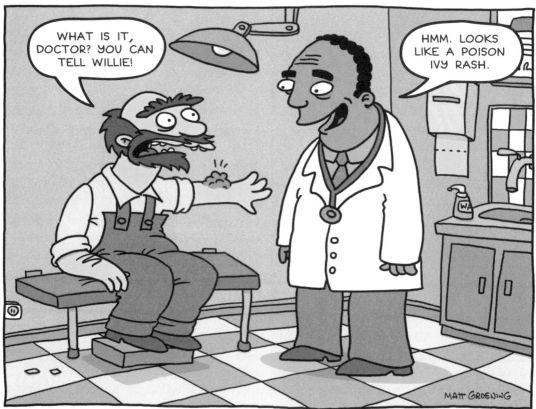

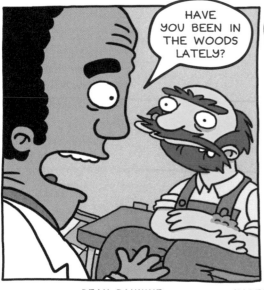

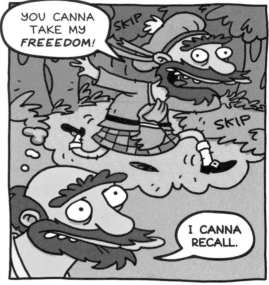

DEAN RANKINE
STORY & ART

KAREN BATES
LETTERS

BILL MORRISON
EDITOR

I RECOMMEND THIS CREAM.
ITCHEZE
PRO
DO IT, DOCTOR! GREASE UP WILLIE!
HOP!
RRIIIPPP
ACTUALLY, IT JUST NEEDS TO BE APPLIED TO THE INFECTED AREA.
SEEMS LIKE YOU HAVE A CASE OF BEING A LITTLE RASH!
HEE HEE HE
?
THE END

SPRINGFIELD VANISHING POINT
VOTED FOURTH BEST MAKE-OUT SPOT IN THE CITY
-SPRINGFIELD SHOPPER
OH, PROFESSOR FRINK!
PLEASE, MISS STELLA, CALL ME JOHN! PROFESSOR FRINK WAS MY FATHER'S NAME!
SHALL I CONTINUE EXPLAINING HEISENBERG'S UNCERTAINTY PRINCIPLE?
WELL, I'M CERTAIN ABOUT ONE THING! COME HERE, YOU!
ER...WELL... ALL RIGHT!
JUST GIVE ME A SECOND TO FRESHEN MY BREATH! IT IS A BIT NERDY!
YOU DON'T NEED THAT!
TOSS!
I LOVE YOU FOR WHO YOU ARE!
COOL JUICE
SMOOCH!
SMAK!
GA-HEY!
SPRINGFIELD WATER SUPPLY
NO MOONSHINE OR NUCLEAR WASTE DUMPING!

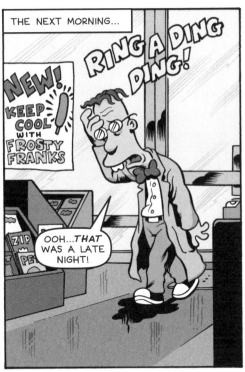

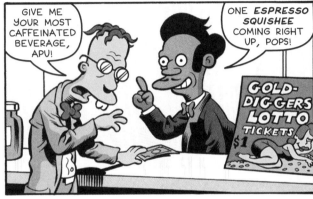

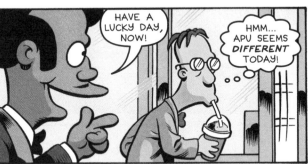

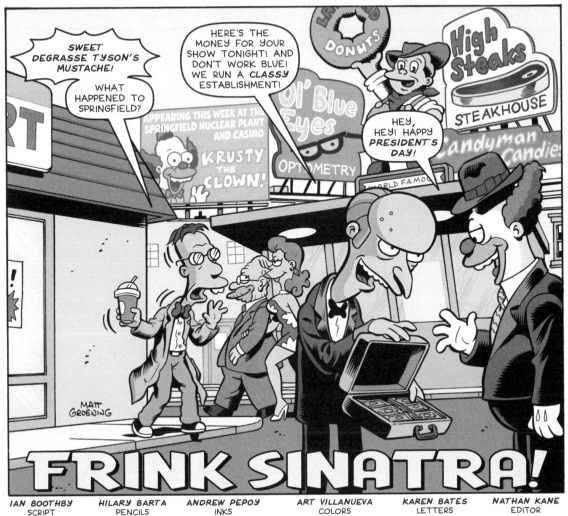

IAN BOOTHBY
SCRIPT

HILARY BARTA
PENCILS

ANDREW PEPOY
INKS

ART VILLANUEVA
COLORS

KAREN BATES
LETTERS

NATHAN KANE
EDITOR

BARNEY! BABE! IT'S NINE O'CLOCK IN THE A.M.! AIN'T THAT A LITTLE EARLY FOR A MARTINI?
MY **WATCH** SAYS FIVE P.M.
IT MUST BE BROKEN! YOU SHOULD GET IT FIXED!
IF I DID THAT, HOW COULD I **DRINK** AT NINE IN THE MORNING?
EXCUSE ME, GENTLEMEN! WHY ARE YOU BEHAVING SO PECULIARLY?
D'OH-RE-MI! LOOK WHAT THE **SPACE PROGRAM** DRAGGED IN!
I'M JUST FOOLIN', CHARLEY! I WAS A LOSER LIKE YOU UNTIL I HAD MY FIRST CUP OF JOE THIS MORNING! NOW **CUCUMBERS** ASK **ME** FOR ADVICE ON BEING COOL!
HOLY FREON! MY **FORMULA** MUST HAVE ENDED UP IN THE WATER SUPPLY!
JUST GRAB A DRINK AND YOU CAN JOIN THE PARTY. I'M THE **CHAIRMAN OF THE BOARD** OF THE GROUP!
YEAH, HE'S THE **CHAIRMAN**, AND WE'RE ALL **BORED!**
I'VE GOT TO CHANGE THE TOWN BACK TO NORMAL!
YOU HEAR THAT?
HE WANTS US TO TAKE THE FIRST TRAIN BACK TO **SQUARESVILLE!**
GET THAT NERD!

LOOK! LANA TURNER!
WHAT? WHERE?
HUBBA HUBBA!
I ⁝WHEEZE⁝ HAVE TO HIDE ⁝GASP⁝ IN THE ONE PLACE A COOL PERSON WOULD NEVER GO...
"...THE SPRINGFIELD PUBLIC LIBRARY!"
SPRINGFIELD PUBLIC LIBRARY
I SAID, "FREEZE!"
AAAAH!
DON'T SHOOT! LEAD IS VERY BAD FOR MY CEREBRAL CORTEX!
HE'S ONE OF US!
DON'T WORRY! THIS IS JUST A LASER TOY I BOUGHT FOR MY CAT MS. MITTENS BEFORE THE TOWN WENT MAD!
WHAT'S HAPPENED, PROFESSOR?

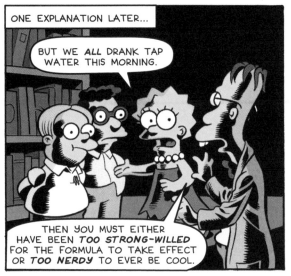

ONE EXPLANATION LATER...

BUT WE *ALL* DRANK TAP WATER THIS MORNING.

THEN YOU MUST EITHER HAVE BEEN *TOO STRONG-WILLED* FOR THE FORMULA TO TAKE EFFECT OR *TOO NERDY* TO EVER BE COOL.

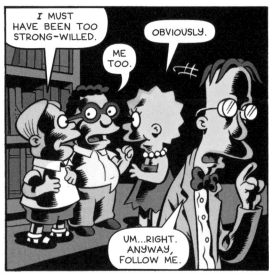

I MUST HAVE BEEN TOO STRONG-WILLED.

ME TOO.

OBVIOUSLY.

UM...RIGHT. ANYWAY, FOLLOW ME.

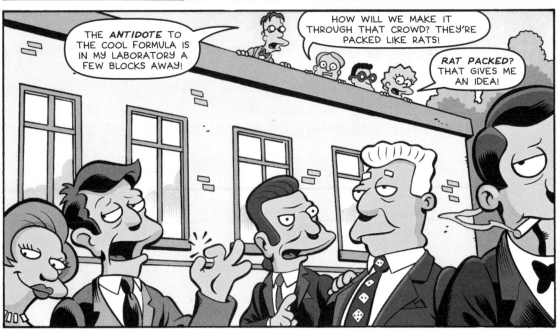

THE *ANTIDOTE* TO THE COOL FORMULA IS IN MY LABORATORY A FEW BLOCKS AWAY!

HOW WILL WE MAKE IT THROUGH THAT CROWD? THEY'RE PACKED LIKE RATS!

RAT PACKED? THAT GIVES ME AN IDEA!

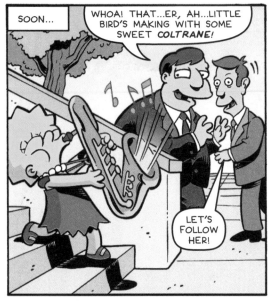

SOON...

WHOA! THAT...ER, AH...LITTLE BIRD'S MAKING WITH SOME SWEET *COLTRANE!*

LET'S FOLLOW HER!

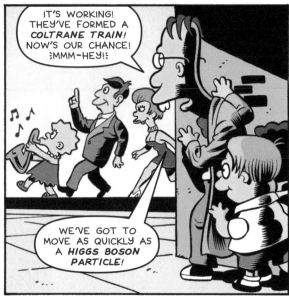

IT'S WORKING! THEY'VE FORMED A *COLTRANE TRAIN!* NOW'S OUR CHANCE! ♪MMM-HEY!♪

WE'VE GOT TO MOVE AS QUICKLY AS A *HIGGS BOSON PARTICLE!*

WIENER TAKE ALL
MAN, THAT CHICKADEE CAN SWING!
PLAY SOME BRUBECK!
OH! I LOVE DAVE BRUBECK! DID YOU KNOW HE RECORDED "TAKE FIVE" IN 5/4 TIME, WHICH WAS BOTH GROUNDBREAKING AND WHERE THE NAME OF THE SONG CAME FROM?
Cats Amore KITTY BOUTIQUE
SHE'S A NERD!
GET HER!
AAAAH! I THOUGHT YOU WERE DISTRACTING THEM!
MY BROTHER BLEW MY COVER!
HA! YOU MELVINS BETTER RUN IN 5/4 TIME!
IT'S NO USE!

IT'S MY JOB TO ROOT OUT SQUARES LIKE YOU!
GIMME THOSE GLASSES!
WHAT TH--?!
HE WAS TALKING ABOUT SQUARE ROOTS! HE'S ONE OF US!
HUH? NO!
PRETEND TO BE COOL, WILL YA? WHY, YOU LITTLE--!
AAAAH!
FRINK LABORATORIES
WE MADE IT! IT MUST HAVE BEEN HARD FOR YOU, LISA, TO TURN ON YOUR BROTHER.
EH, NOT REALLY. NO.
QUICK! GET INSIDE!
CHILDREN! MAKE WITH THE GRABBING OF THE ANTI-DOTE! IT'S BETWEEN THE MARSHMALLOWS AND THE CYBER-MONKEYS!
EXIT

SORRY TO PUT THE KIBOSH ON THIS PARTY, PROF, BUT IT'S LAST CALL!
PLEASE DON'T START WITH THE HITTING, MR. LARGE-TYPE PERSON!
EXIT
HA! YOU MAKE ME LAUGH, PAL!
I DON'T KNOW WHY, BUT I THINK WE COULD HAVE BEEN A GOOD TEAM. MAYBE EVEN PARTNERS!
EXIT
OH WELL! HERE'S A JOKE I HEARD AT A ROAST ONCE! WHAT DID YOUR FACE SAY TO MY FIST?
BEATS ME!
EXACTLY!
GULP!
NOW, SAY HELLO TO MY FRIEND IRMA!
RUN, PROFESSOR!
I'M TOO SCARED!
DO NOT FEED
BRAAAP!
OH, IT HURTS WORSE THAN I EXPECTED!

WHERE AM I?
I SLIPPED SOME OF THE ANTIDOTE INTO MR. GUMBLE'S MARTINI!
THIS MUST BE VERY CONFUSING FOR YOU, WAKING UP WITH NO MEMORY OF WHAT HAPPENED AND HOLDING A DRINK!
ACTUALLY, MOST OF MY MORNINGS START THIS WAY!
OH NO! THE HIPSTERS! THEY'RE GETTING IN!
CRACK!
NO, THEY ALREADY ARE IN! UP AGAINST THIS WALL, POINDEXTERS!
DO WHAT HE SAYS! HE HAS A SLING-SHOT!
BART! BEHIND YOU! A NERD!
HA! EAT SLINGSHOT, DWEEB!
SMASH!
YAAAAH!
YOINK!
THAT'S SEVEN YEARS BAD LUCK FOR YOU...

...HOPEFULLY, IT MEANS GOOD LUCK FOR ME!
I'LL JUST REPLACE THIS RUBBER BAND WITH MY PATENTED FLEXI-FRINK SUPERBAND...
...AND USE THE FORMULA TO SEED THE CLOUDS ABOVE THE CITY!
TWANG!
ROOF
SOON...
FRINK
ABS
IT'S COMING DOWN LIKE A DOZEN OCEANS!
EH...MORE LIKE ELEVEN.
LOOKS LIKE THE PARTY'S OVER!
HUH? WHAT'S GOIN' ON? WHERE ARE WE?
WHO CARES! IT'S AFTER NINE, AND WE'RE NOT AT WORK. WOO-HOO!
FRINK
YOU DID IT, PROFESSOR!
SO IT APPEARS. NOW, IF YOU'LL EXCUSE ME...

MISS STELLA! OUR LATE NIGHT EXPLORATION OF UNIFICATION THEORY NEARLY LED TO THE DEMISE OF THE ENTIRE TOWN!
OUR LOVE IS FAR TOO DANGEROUS. WE MUST MAKE LIKE A ZYGOTE AND SPLIT UP!
I UNDERSTAND! THIS IS WHO YOU ARE AND WHY I'LL LOVE YOU FOREVER!
NOW, IF YOU'LL EXCUSE ME, I'M GOING TO SEE IF BILL NYE THE SCIENCE GUY IS STILL SINGLE!
GA-HOY!
NO WAY
SUPER M
AND LATER THAT NIGHT...
I DON'T REMEMBER WHY I HIRED YOU, BUT I FOUND THIS SIGNED CONTRACT ON MY DESK. A DEAL IS A DEAL...OR SO MY LAWYERS TELL ME.
WHATEVER YOU SAY, METHUSELAH!
Contract
AND SO...
HEY HEY! IS IT HOT IN HERE, OR IS IT JUST THE PLUTONIUM RODS?
WHAT'S THE DEAL? DO YOU ALL GO TO THE SAME TAILOR?
COME ON, GUYS... I'M DYING UP HERE. AT LEAST THAT'S WHAT THE RADIATION DETECTOR SAYS! HEY-O!
NO SWIMMING
IT'S ENDSVILLE, DADDY-O!

THE BEST
RADIOACTIVE™ MAN
EVENT EVER!
PART 1
IT'S FINALLY HERE...
THIS YEAR'S *EVENT* WE'VE ALL BEEN WAITING FOR...
SHHH, YOU GUYS, I'M READING...
RADIOACTIVE MAN
RADIOACTIVE MAN
MATT GROENING
RADIOACTIVE MAN
RADIOACTIVE MAN

BATTON **LASH** SCRIPT · TONE **RODRIGUEZ** PENCILS · ANDREW **PEPOY** INKS · ART **VILLANUEVA** COLORS · KAREN **BATES** LETTERS · BILL **MORRISON** EDITOR

EEP?
EEP! EEEP!
EEP!
EEP EEP EEPP EPP!
EEP, EEP...!

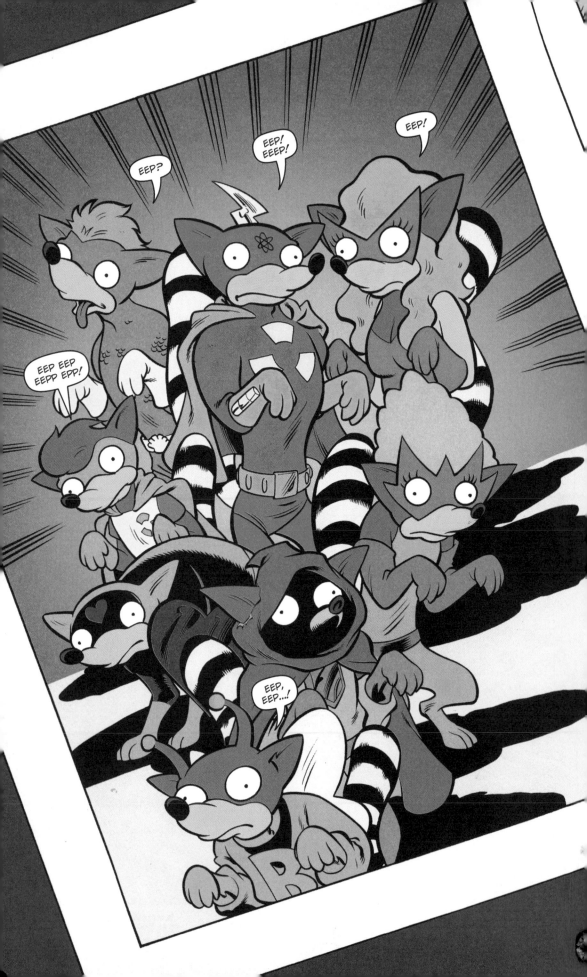

YOU'RE IN BIG TROUBLE NOW, DR. CRAB! HERE COMES THE SUPERIOR-LEMUR SQUAD!
THEY'LL STOP YOU, BUT GOOD!
LET ZEM DO ZEIR VORST, GLORIA GRAND--
HEY, I APPRECIATE THE SAVE, BUT DON'T YOU THINK YOU WERE A TAD EXTREME WITH DR. CRAB--
QUIET, HUMAN!
EEP?
WHOOM!
FOOLS! YOU HAD NO IDEA THAT ALL THIS TIME YOUR WORLD HAS BEEN INFILTRATED BY KRULLERS!
ULTIMATELY, THE SUPERIOR-LEMUR SQUAD ARE JUST A BUNCH OF NOISY ANIMALS, WHILE WE KRULLERS ARE AN ADVANCED ALIEN--
EEP!
EEP!
EEP!
EEP!
EEP!
EEP!
EEP!

WHAT IS THIS?? WHAT'S HAPPENING TO YOU?!?
BRAINS...
YOU--YOU'VE BECOME A *ZOMBIE!* NO...NO!
YAAARGGH!
IS IT JUST ME, OR DOES THIS SUCK?
RADIOACTIVE MAN
RADIOACTIVE MAN

THESE EVENTS IN COMICS JUST AIN'T CUTTING IT ANYMORE!
I AM INCLINED TO AGREE WITH YOU, BART...
...THIS SUMMER'S SUPERIOR-LEMUR SQUAD STORYLINE PALES IN LIGHT OF LAST WINTER'S, WHEN THE SQUAD WERE PANDAS!
AND WHERE DID THE KRULLER COME FROM? I THOUGHT THEIR PLANET WAS OBLITERATED IN LAST YEAR'S "KARMAGEDDON!"
BUT, BART, DIDN'T YOU READ THE LATEST ISSUE OF "LURE LASS"?
IF YOU DID, YOU'D HAVE LEARNED THAT A SPACE ARK WAS LAUNCHED FROM THE KRULLERS' DOOMED PLANET.
THAT WAS HINTED AT IN CAPTAIN SQUID #147!
RADIO
REMEMBER BRAD BRADLEY, LURE LASS'S LONG-TIME LOVE?
BRAD TURNED OUT TO BE A KRULLER!
WHEN DID THAT HAPPEN??
THAT WAS CHRONICLED IN BUG BOY ANNUAL SPECIAL #5!

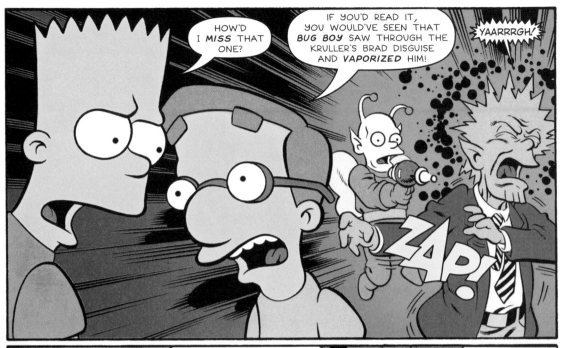

HOW'D I *MISS* THAT ONE?

IF YOU'D READ IT, YOU WOULD'VE SEEN THAT *BUG BOY* SAW THROUGH THE KRULLER'S BRAD DISGUISE AND *VAPORIZED* HIM!

YAARRRGH!

ZAP!

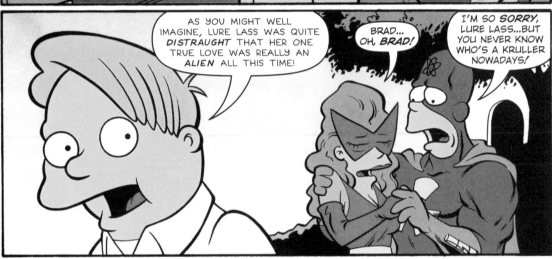

AS YOU MIGHT WELL IMAGINE, LURE LASS WAS QUITE *DISTRAUGHT* THAT HER ONE TRUE LOVE WAS REALLY AN *ALIEN* ALL THIS TIME!

BRAD... OH, *BRAD!*

I'M SO *SORRY,* LURE LASS...BUT YOU NEVER KNOW WHO'S A KRULLER NOWADAYS!

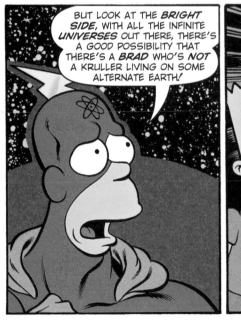

BUT LOOK AT THE *BRIGHT SIDE*, WITH ALL THE INFINITE *UNIVERSES* OUT THERE, THERE'S A GOOD POSSIBILITY THAT THERE'S A *BRAD* WHO'S *NOT* A KRULLER LIVING ON SOME ALTERNATE EARTH!

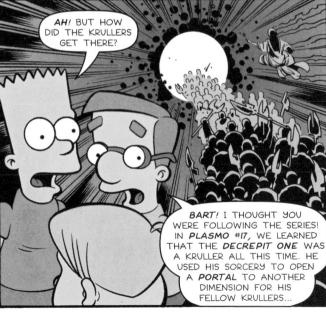

AH! BUT HOW DID THE KRULLERS GET THERE?

BART! I THOUGHT YOU WERE FOLLOWING THE SERIES! IN *PLASMO #17,* WE LEARNED THAT THE *DECREPIT ONE* WAS A KRULLER ALL THIS TIME. HE USED HIS SORCERY TO OPEN A *PORTAL* TO ANOTHER DIMENSION FOR HIS FELLOW KRULLERS...

YOU ARE AWARE THAT LURE LASS NEVER FOUND A NEW BRAD, RIGHT? DIDN'T YOU READ WEASEL WOMAN #34?
I GAVE UP ON THE STORY AFTER IT CONTINUED IN BRAVE HEART #89 ...I COULDN'T AFFORD ALL THE TITLES!
DUDE! I THOUGHT I WAS KEEPING UP WITH IT! WHAT ELSE DID I MISS?
LET'S SEE...IT STARTED IN THAT THE RAVE & THE RAD TEAM-UP ONE SHOT FEATURING PLASMO AND FALLOUT BOY...
...THAT LED INTO RADIOACTIVE MAN #1075...
...THAT CONTINUED IN SUPERIOR SQUAD #229...
...THAT LED INTO CAPT. SQUID #148...
...WHICH CONTINUED IN SUPERIOR SQUAD #230...
...WHICH SEGUED INTO THE BUGBOY ANNUAL...
...THAT CONTINUED ON IN--
HEY! DON'T YOU GUYS WANNA HEAR WHAT HAPPENED?
MAYBE SOME OTHER TIME, MILHOUSE.
YES! LET'S KICK BACK WITH SOME STRAIGHTFORWARD ENTERTAINMENT AND UNCOMPLICATED VIOLENCE!
WHOOM!
AIIEE!
BANG BANG BANG!

HEY, HEY, HEY! THIS IS NO GAME, PEOPLE..
...SO LISTEN UP. TELL 'EM THE BAD NEWS, MISS PENNYCANDY.
SALES ARE DOWN THIS QUARTER...FOR THE FOURTH TIME IN A ROW! IT'S BAD ENOUGH THAT THE FLAGSHIP TITLE, "RADIOACTIVE MAN," HAS SLIPPED...
...BUT ITS DECLINE HAS AFFECTED THE OTHER TITLES AS WELL!
SUPERIOR SQUAD
CAPT. SQUID
AS THE NEW OWNER AND PUBLISHER OF "RADIOACTIVE MAN" COMICS, MY GOAL IS TO BEAT THE PANTS OFF THE COMPETITION!
THAT'S RIGHT, FELLAS, I WON A COMIC BOOK COMPANY IN LAST NIGHT'S POKER GAME!
YEAH, BUT IT PUBLISHES "RADIOACTIVE MAN"!
SNICKER!
WHAT'S WRONG WITH THAT?
KIDS THINK THE CHARACTER'S CORNY!
MY COMPANY PUBLISHES "TRAPEZOID MAN"...THAT'S WHAT THE FANS LIKE!
TO THE KIDS OF TODAY, "RADIOACTIVE MAN" IS SOMETHING THEIR PARENTS READ!

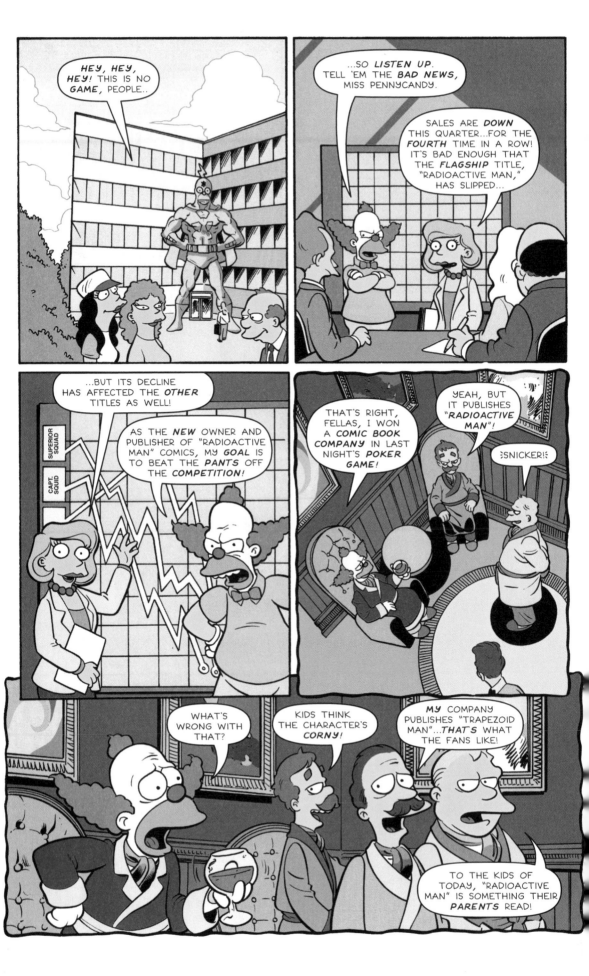

TOUGH LUCK, KRUSTY!
YOU THOUGHT YOU ACQUIRED A SUPER-HERO, BUT YOU GOT STUCK WITH A WHITE ELEPHANT!
HAW HAW HAW!
LISTEN TO ME, PEOPLE...
...WE NEED TO PUT OUR HEADS TOGETHER AND THINK.
MY ASSISTANT, MISS PENNYCANDY, HAS ALL THE RECORDS, MEMOS, AND SALES CHARTS OF THE LAST THIRTY YEARS SO WE CAN DETERMINE THE TRENDS AND READER REACTION TO MANUFACTURED EVENTS.
WE'RE NOT LEAVING THIS BOARDROOM UNTIL YOU COME UP WITH A STORYLINE THAT WILL PUMP NEW LIFE INTO THIS 50-YEAR-OLD PROPERTY AND HAVE EVERYONE TALKING ABOUT RADIOACTIVE MAN AGAIN WITH SALES THAT WILL KICK TRAPEZOID MAN'S BUTT!
YES, SIR!
NOW, LET'S ORDER IN AND GET TO WORK!
YES, SIR!

AND SO...
WOK-KING DUCK CHINESE FOOD
KRUSTY BURGER
WHY DON'T WE **KILL OFF** RADIOACTIVE MAN?
MISS PENNYCANDY...?
BEEN THERE, DONE THAT!
THEN HOW ABOUT WE JUST **BREAK HIS BACK**?
HOW ABOUT THAT, PENNYCANDY?
HMM...I SEE THAT WORKED **15 YEARS AGO**. IN FACT, IT WAS **SO** SUCCESSFUL...

...THE COMPANY BROKE A DIFFERENT BODY PART FOR **ALL** THEIR CHARACTERS, UNTIL THEY RAN OUT OF BODY PARTS...
...AND **CHARACTERS!**
I'VE **GOT** **IT!** HOW ABOUT IF RADIOACTIVE MAN **QUITS?**
I WAS A **YOUNG MAN** WHEN I FIRST BECAME **RADIOACTIVE MAN,**
AND EVERY BOY, SOONER OR LATER, WILL PUT AWAY HIS TOYS...
...AND IF HE'S **LUCKY,** HE CAN GO BACK TO BEING A **PLAYBOY** FULL-TIME!

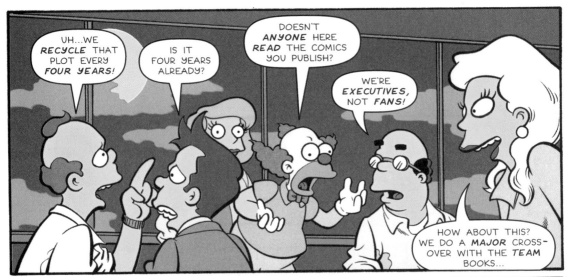

UH...WE *RECYCLE* THAT PLOT EVERY *FOUR YEARS!*

IS IT FOUR YEARS ALREADY?

DOESN'T *ANYONE* HERE *READ* THE COMICS YOU PUBLISH?

WE'RE *EXECUTIVES,* NOT *FANS!*

HOW ABOUT THIS? WE DO A *MAJOR* CROSS-OVER WITH THE *TEAM* BOOKS...

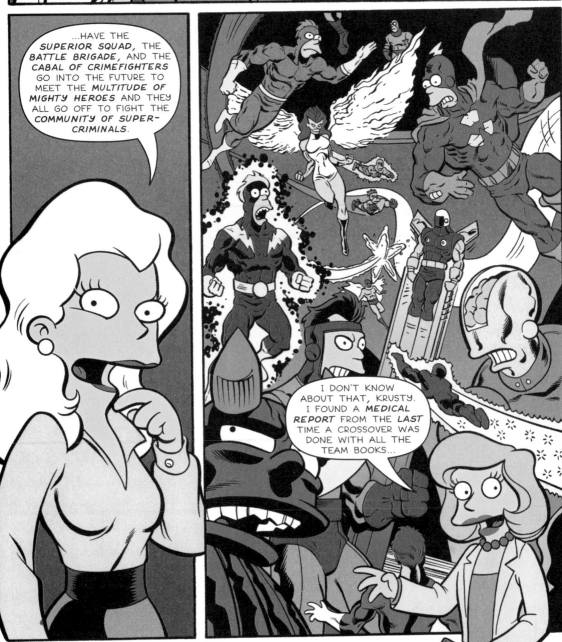

...HAVE THE *SUPERIOR SQUAD,* THE *BATTLE BRIGADE,* AND THE *CABAL OF CRIMEFIGHTERS* GO INTO THE FUTURE TO MEET THE *MULTITUDE OF MIGHTY HEROES* AND THEY ALL GO OFF TO FIGHT THE *COMMUNITY OF SUPER-CRIMINALS.*

I DON'T KNOW ABOUT THAT, KRUSTY. I FOUND A *MEDICAL REPORT* FROM THE *LAST* TIME A CROSSOVER WAS DONE WITH ALL THE TEAM BOOKS...

"...THE PENCILLER AND INKER STILL HAVEN'T RECOVERED!"
STRONG LASS... BULB BOY...EH...EH... DYNAMO LAD, THUNDER THIGHS...EH...EH...
THE ROLL CALL NEVER ENDS...EH...EH... IT NEVER ENDS!!
OKAY, THEN... HOW ABOUT WE CHANGE RADIOACTIVE MAN'S COSTUME?
WHAT, AGAIN? EVEN I KNOW THAT'S BEEN DONE...
"...FIRST IN THE '70s..."
"...THEN IN THE '80s..."
...AND THE '90s! AND I OUGHTA KNOW...EACH TIME YOUR COMPANY PULLED THIS STUNT, THEY HIRED A HIMBO MODEL TO HYPE IT ON MY TV SHOW!
YES, I REMEMBER.

YOU KNOW, KRUSTY, MAYBE WE SHOULD CALL IN SOME PEOPLE ON THE CREATIVE STAFF AND ASK **THEM** FOR IDEAS.
WHAT?!? DON'T YOU THINK ***MANAGEMENT*** KNOWS BETTER?
YOU DON'T ***TRUST*** A CREATIVE PERSON WITH AN IMPORTANT DECISION LIKE A STORYLINE! WHAT'S ***WRONG*** WITH YOU, MAN?!?
TCH!
I-I MUST'VE LOST MY HEAD. I'M ***SORRY***!
LOOK. YOUR JOBS ARE ON THE LINE IF WE DON'T COME UP WITH SOMETHING THAT WILL CAPTURE THE ***IMAGINATION*** AND EMPTY THE ***WALLETS*** OF FANS ***EVERYWHERE***!
COMES THE DAWN AND COUNTLESS TIRED IDEAS LATER...
WE ***TRIED*** OUR ***BEST***, KRUSTY!
BUT APPARENTLY IT WASN'T ***GOOD*** ENOUGH!
IT'S NOT OUR ***FAULT***, KRUSTY!
THE PROBLEM IS WITH THE ***FANS***!
YEAH! THEY WANT SOMETHING ***NEW*** ALL THE TIME...
...BUT DEMAND THINGS ***STAY*** THE SAME!
NOTHING WE ANNOUNCE COULD LIVE UP TO THEIR PRECONCEIVED EXPECTATIONS!
FEH! MISS PENNYCANDY, SEND IN MS. NAEGLE.

WHILE YOU HAVE BEEN WRACKING YOUR BRAINS TRYING TO REPEAT YESTERDAY'S CONCEPTS, I ASKED LINDSEY NAEGLE IN OUR SALES AND MARKETING DEPARTMENT TO COME UP WITH AN IDEA TO APPEAL TO TODAY'S READER.
I WAS NEVER ONE FOR FALSE MODESTY, SO I'LL JUST COME RIGHT OUT AND SAY THIS IS A BRILLANT SOLUTION TO OUR PROBLEM.
THIS COMP I WHIPPED UP SHOWS YOU THE ONLY WAY FANS CAN HAVE BOTH THE OLD AND THE NEW!
GASP!
AWESOME IN ITS SIMPLICITY!
I THINK IT'S GOING TO BE THE NEXT STEP IN COMICS PUBLISHING!
CAN WE DO THAT?!?
LINDSEY, IT'S SO DARING AN APPROACH... HOW DO WE PROMOTE IT TO GET EVERYONE TO BUY IT WITHOUT TURNING THEM OFF?
WE'RE GOING TO PROMOTE IT BY SAYING NOTHING!

REMEMBER THE GOOD OLD DAYS, BART?
WE COULDN'T WAIT FOR THE NEW ISSUE OF "RADIOACTIVE MAN" TO COME OUT. BUT NOW...!
I HEAR YOU, MILHOUSE! WE'RE JUST GOING THROUGH THE MOTIONS!
YOU DARE NOT MISS THE AMAZING STORY OF "RADIOACTIVE MAN- RIGHT" AND "RADIOACTIVE MAN -LEFT"!
I REMEMBER THE FIRST SIGN OF A DECLINE IN QUALITY...IT WAS WHEN I FOUND A MINT-SLASH-VERY GOOD COPY OF RADIOACTIVE MAN #132, FROM 1963 AT THE ANDRIOD'S DUNGEON...
"...AND THE SAME PLOT WAS RE-USED IN THE LATEST ISSUE OF RADIOACTIVE MAN IN THAT WEEK'S NEW COMICS!"
PRIVATE SECTOR!
PUBLIC SERVICE!

IT WAS BAD ENOUGH THAT THE "TWO-PARTY RADIOACTIVE MAN" STORYLINE CARRIED OVER TO FIFTY DIFFERENT TITLES...
...BUT ALL THEY DID WAS ARGUE WITH ANYONE WHO DISAGREED WITH THEM!
WAR MONGER!
APPEASER!
SEXIST!
FEMINAZI!
I'LL SQUASH YOU LIKE THE BUG YOU ARE!
THAT'S AN INSECTIST REMARK, HYPNO-HEAD!
POLLUTER!
HOW'D YOU LIKE MY CARBON FOOTPRINT ON YOUR BUTT?
SOME "EVENT!"

HOMER, HAVE YOU NOTICED BART'S BEEN AWFULLY MOODY LATELY?
WHO? YEAH, I GUESS.
NOT TO WORRY, MOM...
...BART IS JUST A LITTLE UPSET OVER THE CURRENT STORYLINES IN HIS COMICS. HE'S TIRED OF BUYING ALL THE TIE-INS AND GETTING NO PAY-OFF!
BART STARTED TO TELL ME HOW THE COMIC BOOK COMPANIES ARE RUINING HIS CHARACTERS, BUT I TUNED OUT.
AH, YOUTH! TO FRITTER AWAY THEIR TIME ON SUCH TRIVAL CONCERNS! WHEN HE GROWS UP, HE'LL SEE THERE ARE MORE IMPORTANT THINGS TO WORRY ABOUT AND--
WHAT?! THE ISOTOPES ARE TRADING AWAY BUCK MITCHELL? WHAT...ARE THEY NUTS?! WHY, THOSE NO GOOD...!
MITCHELL'S THE BEST SECOND BASEMAN THE ISOTOPES EVER HAD! I SHOULD BOYCOTT THEIR CRUMMY BALL CLUB! I OUGHTA--!
DAD! DON'T GET SO WORKED UP! WHAT'S DONE IS DONE!
WELL, ACTUALLY, LISA, IT'S NOT DONE! IT'S JUST A RUMOR! BUT STILL...! IF THE ISOTOPES TRADE HIM AWAY, THEY'RE JERKS!
:SIGH!: DAD, WHY DON'T YOU SEE IF THERE'S ANYTHING ABOUT THIS ON THE NEWS?
REMEMBER, EVERYONE, DINNER, LIKE THE NEWS, WILL BE READY AT SIX.

"THE WAR IS WINDING DOWN, THE ECONOMY IS UP, UNEMPLOYMENT IS DOWN...GROAN! I HATE A SLOW NEWS DAY!"
CHANNEL 6
YOU'D THINK A TRAGEDY WOULD OCCUR, BUT NOOOO! WHAT AM I GOING TO DO FOR A JUICY LEAD FOR TONIGHT'S BROADCAST?
HELLO! WHAT'S THIS...?
"A DARING NEW APPROACH FOR A POP CULTURE ICON," EH? I GUESS THIS WILL HAVE TO DO. AFTER ALL, I'M A VETERAN JOURNALIST...
...I THINK I KNOW A LITTLE SOMETHING ABOUT MAKING A BIG DEAL OUT OF NOTHING!
A LIDDLE MORE WEECH HAZEL, MEESTER BROCKMAN?
PRESENTLY...
CHANGE
CHANNEL 6
...THE FOLLOWING STORY JUST BEGS TO ASK THE QUESTION: IS NOTHING SACRED? THE PUBLISHERS OF THE VENERABLE "RADIOACTIVE MAN" COMICS PROMISES A FRESH DIRECTION FOR THE CHARACTER...

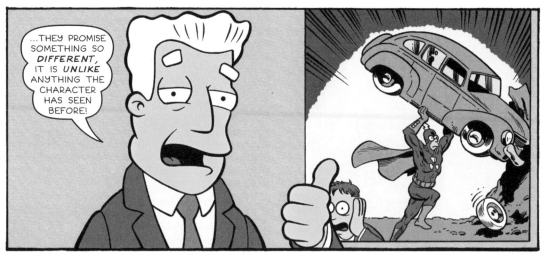

...THEY PROMISE SOMETHING SO *DIFFERENT,* IT IS *UNLIKE* ANYTHING THE CHARACTER HAS SEEN BEFORE!

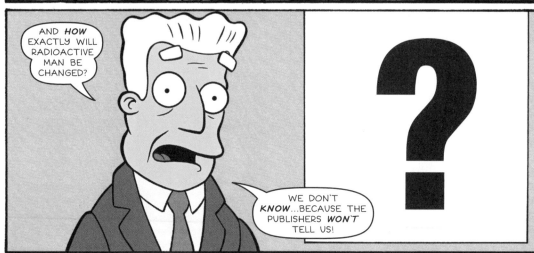

AND *HOW* EXACTLY WILL RADIOACTIVE MAN BE CHANGED?

WE DON'T *KNOW*...BECAUSE THE PUBLISHERS *WON'T* TELL US!

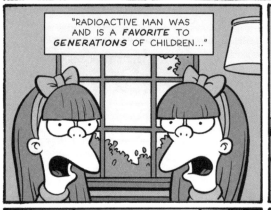

"RADIOACTIVE MAN WAS AND IS A *FAVORITE* TO *GENERATIONS* OF CHILDREN..."

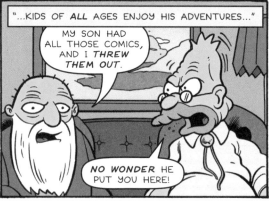

"...KIDS OF *ALL* AGES ENJOY HIS ADVENTURES..."

MY SON HAD ALL THOSE COMICS, AND I *THREW THEM OUT.*

NO WONDER HE PUT YOU HERE!

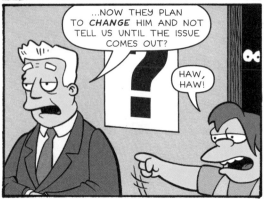

...NOW THEY PLAN TO *CHANGE* HIM AND NOT TELL US UNTIL THE ISSUE COMES OUT?

HAW, HAW!

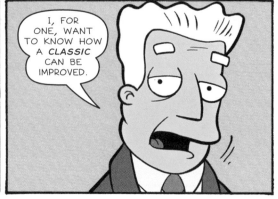

I, FOR ONE, WANT TO KNOW HOW A *CLASSIC* CAN BE IMPROVED.

DO WE REALLY *WANT* TO SEE OUR BELOVED HERO CHANGED FOR THE SAKE OF CHANGE FOR A CHEAP PROMOTIONAL CAMPAIGN THAT WILL TRAMPLE ON *YEARS* OF *TRADITION* JUST TO SELL A FEW EXTRA COPIES?
BUT IF THERE'S A *CHANCE* THAT THIS MIGHT INDEED BE A ONCE-IN-A LIFETIME *COLLECTOR'S ITEM*...
Duff

...I GUESS IT WOULD BE WISE TO PURCHASE MULTIPLE COPIES OF THE NEW "RADIOACTIVE MAN." WHO KNOWS? YOU MIGHT BE ABLE TO SELL THEM AT AN INFLATED PRICE AND PAY FOR YOUR KID'S COLLEGE TUITION.
...NO, BILL, I HAVE NO INTENTION OF PLACING AN ADVANCE RE-ORDER--
PARDON ME?
PLEASE DO NOT OPEN THE TOYS
IF YOU ARE SO INCLINED, RUN DON'T WALK TO YOUR LOCAL COMIC BOOK STORE. THIS IS KENT BROCKMAN SAYING "UP AND ATOM!"...OR WORDS TO THAT EFFECT.
OF COURSE I AM WATCHING THE NEWS...DO YOU THINK I LIVE IN A VACUUM?
I FIND IT DELICIOUSLY IRONIC THAT WHEN I WISHED TO CONTACT YOU, MY REP AT ZIRCON DISTRIBUTORS, TO REPLACE SEVERAL COMICS THAT ARRIVED DAMAGED IN LAST WEEK'S SHIPMENT, I NEVER RECEIVED A CALL BACK...
...BUT NOW, BECAUSE THERE IS A LITTLE ITEM ON THE NEWS ABOUT *YAWN* RADIOACTIVE MAN, YOU HAVE SEEN FIT TO GIVE ME A "COURTESY CALL" TO SEE IF I WANT TO INCREASE MY ORDERS ON A "HOT" TITLE! THANKS, BUT NO THANKS, BILL.
WHY YOU ASK? PLEASE. DON'T INSULT MY INTELLIGENCE.
YOU MUST THINK I WAS BORN YESTERDAY, BILL.
I AM NOT ONE TO FALL FOR A COMIC BOOK COMPANY'S HYPE, GIMMICKS, OR RELENTLESS SALES PLOYS.
FINAL CRUX
SUPERIOR SQUAD! FINAL CRUX
CRISIS AT WAR
WORLDS IN ANXIETY
IDENTITY CHALLENGED
SUPERIOR SQUAD! IDENTITY CHALLENGED
SUPERIOR SQUAD! CRISIS AT WAR 100 COPIES

I SEE NO NEED TO UP MY ORDERS. IN FACT, I--
HOLD THE LINE, I HAVE CUSTOMERS.
I WANNA ORDER TEN COPIES OF THAT "RADIOACTIVE MAN" COMIC!
I'LL TAKE TEN, TOO!
I'LL TAKE TEN CASES, MAN!
WHO'S THE ARTIST GONNA BE?
WHO'S THE WRITER?
HOW IS THIS GOING TO AFFECT CONTINUITY?
I SAW ON THE NEWS THAT THE CHANGE IS GONNA BE DRASTIC!
WHY WON'T THEY SAY WHAT IT'S GOING BE?

AARRR...DID YOU GET A SNEAK PEEK AT IT?
HOW DIFFERENT CAN IT GET?
I CAN'T WAIT TO CONFISCATE AN ISSUE FROM MY STUDENTS...HOLD FIVE COPIES FOR ME!
WOULD ADVANCE PURCHASE OF THE "RADIO-ACTIVE MAN" PUBLICATION INSURE THE CONTINUATION OF SAID SERIES?
WHO CARES? JUST TELL ME HOW MUCH THE NEW "RADIOACTIVE MAN" IS GONNA BE WORTH!
AY AY AY! ES PERMANENTE EL CAMBIO??
WHERE'S THE NEW DUFFMAN? BRAAAP!
UNO MOMENTO, PLEASE...
BILL, I AM A VERY BUSY MAN. IF IT'LL GET YOU OFF MY PHONE, THEN UP MY ORDER ON THE NEW "RADIOACTIVE MAN"...BY 1000%!
& BASEBALL CARDS DUNGEON
...AND, BILL...I EXPECT ZIRCON TO PAY THE SHIPPING IN LIEU OF MY DAMAGED BOOKS FROM LAST WEEK!
GEE, BART...
...IT LOOKS LIKE EVERYONE IS INTERESTED IN THE NEW "RADIOACTIVE MAN"!
IT'S NICE TO KNOW THAT THE APPEAL OF THE CHARACTER REACHES OUT TO THE GENERAL PUBLIC!
YEAH, WELL, LET'S JUST GET OUR COMICS AND SPLIT.

NOT SO FAST, DUDE! WE WERE HERE FIRST!
YEAH...NO ONE'S GOING IN UNTIL SOME PEOPLE GO OUT!
GUYS, I MISS THE DAYS WHEN ONLY WE CARED ABOUT RADIOACTIVE MAN!
HAS EVERYONE IN SPRINGFIELD FALLEN FOR THE HYPE? WILL BART AND HIS FRIENDS EVENTUALLY BE DUPED BY THIS ARTIFICAL "EVENT"?

WE CAN'T DALLY WHILE THE FORCES OF INJUSTICE MOVE ON, BART! UP AND ATOM!
DON'T HAVE A COW, RADIOACTIVE MAN! I'M RIGHT BEHIND YOU!
MATT GROENING
THE BEST RADIOACTIVE MAN™ EVENT EVER! PART 2

BATTON **LASH** SCRIPT · TONE **RODRIGUEZ** PENCILS · ANDREW **PEPOY** INKS · ART **VILLANUEVA** COLORS · KAREN **BATES** LETTERS · BILL **MORRISON** EDITOR

WATCH OUT, RADIOACTIVE MAN!
DR. CRAB IS RIGHT BEHIND YOU!
THANKS, LITTLE BUDDY... I SEE HIM!
POW!
ACH!
LOOK OUT, BART, WHILE I STOP THIS EVIL ROBOT!
SCRUNCH
GO FOR IT, MAN!

WOW, RADIOACTIVE MAN...THE SUPERIOR SQUAD HEADQUARTERS IS SO COOL!
I GUESS IT IS AT THAT, BART!
SAY! DID I EVER TELL YOU ABOUT THE TIME MY TEAMMATES AND I WHUPPED CONQUERO THE STARFISH?
DON'T WORRY, MS. GRAND...I'LL SAVE YOU!
OH, RADIOACTIVE MAN...YOU'RE WONDERFUL!
HMPH!

WHEN I SAW YOU IN DANGER, MS. GRAND, I REALIZED HOW MUCH I CARE FOR YOU. I MUST ASK YOU...
YES, RADIOACTIVE MAN?
WILL YOU MARRY ME?
OH, RADIOACTIVE MAN! MY ANSWER IS...
YEECH!
EXCUSE ME?
WHAT'S THE PROBLEM, BART?
YOU'RE GETTING MARRIED? DON'T YOU KNOW HOW THAT'S GONNA CHANGE THINGS?
BUT CHANGE IS GOOD, BART! IT'S A PART OF LIFE!
YEAH, WELL, BUT SOMETIMES WHEN THINGS CHANGE FOR THE SAKE OF CHANGING...
BART...?
...THOSE CHANGES TEND TO SUCK!
BART!
EH? YIKES--!
YES, MRS. KRABAPPEL?
I SAID, STOP DAYDREAMING, OPEN YOUR TEXTBOOK, AND PAY ATTENTION!

WHATEVER YOU SAY, MRS. K!
APE AND THE ROBOT!

AND AFTER THE SCHOOL DAY FINALLY ENDS...
WHO CAN CONCENTRATE ON SCHOOL WHEN THE *FUTURE* OF RADIOACTIVE MAN MAY BE AT STAKE?
EVER SINCE IT WAS ANNOUNCED THAT THERE WOULD BE ***CHANGES*** IN THE RADIOACTIVE MAN COMIC, IT'S ALL I CAN ***THINK*** OF!
I SHARE YOUR ***CONCERNS,*** MY FRIENDS...
BUT WHAT IF THE CHANGE IS FOR THE ***BETTER?***

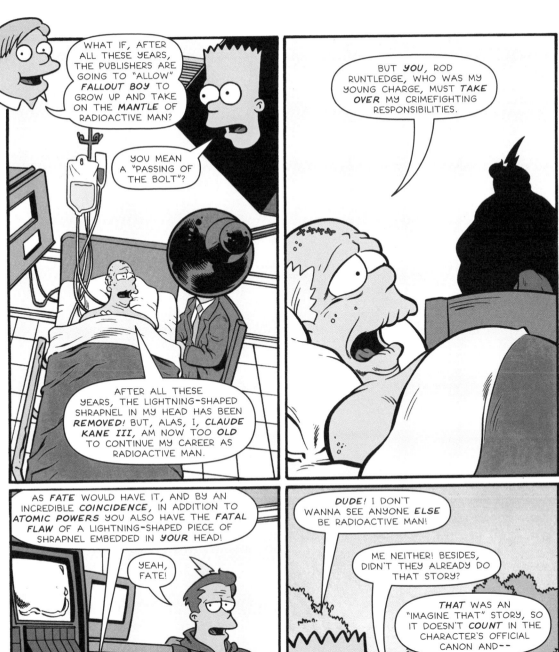

WHAT IF, AFTER ALL THESE YEARS, THE PUBLISHERS ARE GOING TO "ALLOW" *FALLOUT BOY* TO GROW UP AND TAKE ON THE *MANTLE* OF RADIOACTIVE MAN?

YOU MEAN A "PASSING OF THE BOLT"?

AFTER ALL THESE YEARS, THE LIGHTNING-SHAPED SHRAPNEL IN MY HEAD HAS BEEN *REMOVED!* BUT, ALAS, I, *CLAUDE KANE III,* AM NOW TOO *OLD* TO CONTINUE MY CAREER AS RADIOACTIVE MAN.

BUT *YOU,* ROD RUNTLEDGE, WHO WAS MY YOUNG CHARGE, MUST *TAKE OVER* MY CRIMEFIGHTING RESPONSIBILITIES.

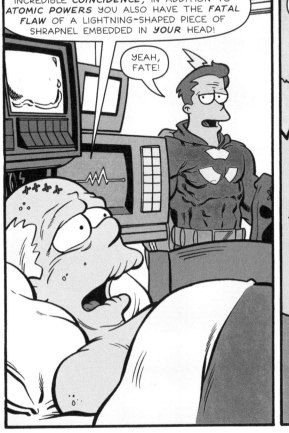

AS *FATE* WOULD HAVE IT, AND BY AN INCREDIBLE *COINCIDENCE,* IN ADDITION TO *ATOMIC POWERS* YOU ALSO HAVE THE *FATAL FLAW* OF A LIGHTNING-SHAPED PIECE OF SHRAPNEL EMBEDDED IN *YOUR* HEAD!

YEAH, FATE!

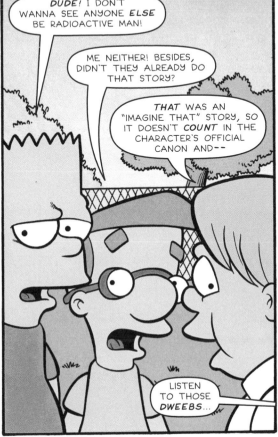

DUDE! I DON'T WANNA SEE ANYONE *ELSE* BE RADIOACTIVE MAN!

ME NEITHER! BESIDES, DIDN'T THEY ALREADY DO THAT STORY?

THAT WAS AN "IMAGINE THAT" STORY, SO IT DOESN'T *COUNT* IN THE CHARACTER'S OFFICIAL CANON AND--

LISTEN TO THOSE *DWEEBS...*

...THEY STILL READ COMICS!
AND THEY TALK ABOUT THEM LIKE IT'S SO IMPORTANT!
I THINK WE OUGHTA BEAT THESE GUYS TO A PULP!
WHATTA BUNCHA LOSERS!
"UP AND ATOM!" YEAH, RIGHT!
HA HA HA!
THEY IDOLIZE A GUY WHO RUNS AROUND IN RED UNDERWEAR!
WAH HA HA HA!
AND...AND A CAPE! HA HA HA!
OKAY, SAPS, WHO'S GONNA CATCH A BEATING FIRST...HUH?
HEY, JIMBO...?
!
WHERE'D THEY GO?!
WHILE WE WERE MOCKING THEM, THEY SPLIT!
HAW HAW!

HI, BART. HOW WAS SCHOOL TODAY?
ANY DAY I GET HOME IN ONE PIECE IS A GOOD ONE, MOM!
THAT'S NICE, DEAR.
HEY, BART, YOU'RE JUST IN TIME.
WHAT'S UP, LISA?
THERE'S SOMETHING ON THE NEWS ABOUT RADIOACTIVE MAN!
THIS IS KENT BROCKMAN, CONTINUING OUR INVESTIGATIVE REPORT ON THE SOON TO BE RELEASED RADIOACTIVE MAN COMIC BOOK...
...AS WE INQUIRE AS TO WHAT CHANGES ARE PLANNED FOR THE VENERABLE COMIC BOOK CHARACTER, AND MORE IMPORTANTLY, WHY ALL THE SECRECY?
I ASKED THE CURRENT OWNER AND PUBLISHER TO COME CLEAN...
NOW WE'LL GET TO THE BOTTOM OF THIS!

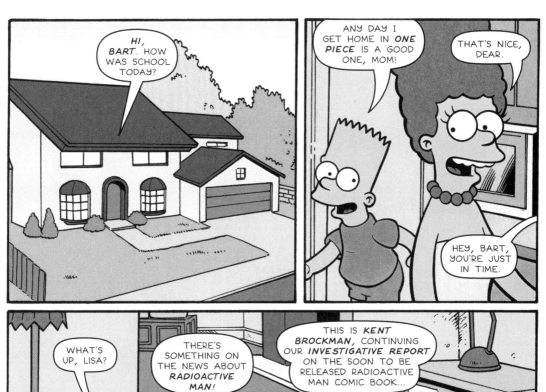

WHEN I ACQUIRED THE RADIOACTIVE MAN PROPERTY, I SAW I HAD A RESPONSIBILITY TO AN AMERICAN ICON, WHICH WAS TO MAKE HIM RELEVANT TO TODAY'S CONSUMERS.
KRUSTY THE CLOWN -TV PERSONALITY/ENTREPRENEUR/SHNORER
ACCORDING TO MY NOTES, YOU "ACQUIRED" THE PROPERTY IN A POKER GAME!
WHO ARE YOU? MIKE WALLACE? I OWN THE CHARACTER NOW, AND LET'S LEAVE IT AT THAT! BESIDES, IT WAS THE ONLY ASSET THAT DEADBEAT PUBLISHER HAD!
OOOKAY... LET'S MOVE ON TO THE CONTROVERSIAL REVAMP YOU'RE PLANNING FOR "RADIOACTIVE MAN."
IT'S UNIQUE IN THE HISTORY OF COMICS THAT THERE IS ABSOLUTELY NO INKLING TO WHAT THE CHANGES WOULD BE OR WHAT FANS ARE TO EXPECT! WHY NO PREVIEW, KRUSTY?
WHASSA MATTER WITH YOU? DONTCHA LIKE SURPRISES?
JUST WAIT FOR THE FARSHLUGINER COMIC TO COME OUT AND SEE FOR YOURSELF! JEEZ!
BUT, KRUSTY, FANS OF ALL AGES ARE WONDERING IF RADIOACTIVE MAN IS GOING TO GET MARRIED, OR GET A NEW COSTUME, OR MEET HIS LONG LOST COUSIN, OR--

HEY, YOU DEAF? I SAID WAIT AND SEE!
BUT A WORD TO THE WISE...YOU BETTER ORDER EXTRA COPIES!
HEH, HEH! WHAT GOES AROUND, COMES AROUND...EH, BOY?
WE'LL BE FOLLOWING THIS STORY AS IT DEVELOPS. UNTIL THEN, "UP AND ATOM!"
WHAT ARE YOU TALKING ABOUT, HOMER?
THIS ISN'T THE FIRST TIME RADIOACTIVE MANIA HAS TAKEN A HOLD OF SPRINGFIELD!
IT ISN'T?
I REMEMBER WHEN I WAS YOUR AGE, AND THE RADIO-ACTIVE MAN TV SHOW CAME ON, EVERYONE WAS INTO IT.
MINION 1
YOU'LL NEVER GET AWAY WITH THIS, MR. KIDNEY PUNCH!
DO NOT BE TOO SURE OF THAT, IRRADIATED CRUSADER. I DO BELIEVE IT IS CURTAINS FOR YOU...

LET US LEAVE, SCARLET FLOOZY, AS OUR ARCH-FOES MEET THEIR MOST UNTIMELY DEMISE!
WHATEVER YOU SAY, PARTNER! "WHEEL" SEE YOU "AROUND," CAPED CRIMEFIGHTERS!
HOLY SPIRALING OUT OF CONTROL, RADIOACTIVE MAN! NOW WHAT?
WHAT NOW, INDEED? IT LOOKS LIKE A TURN FOR THE WORSE FOR OUR HEROES!
BE SURE TO SPIN THE DIAL BACK TO THIS STATION TOMORROW NIGHT. SAME RADIOACTIVE TIME!

BUT THAT SHOW SUCKED!
AW, HOW CAN YOU SAY THAT? IT WAS SO MUCH FUN! AND THEY HAD GUEST STARS LIKE SHELDON LEONARD AS MR. KIDNEY PUNCH AND ARLENE FRANCIS AS THE SCARLET FLOOZY.
SCARLET FLOOZY... MRRAWL!
WHATEVER, HOMER. WHAT GETS ME IS THAT EVERYONE IS JUMPING ON THE RADIOACTIVE MAN BANDWAGON, BUT WHAT ABOUT THE LONGTIME FANS?
WELL, BART, IF YOU'RE UPSET BY THE CHANGES IN "RADIOACTIVE MAN," YOU SHOULD BE PROACTIVE AND PROTEST THE CHANGES!
BUT THAT'S THE PROBLEM, LIS...I DON'T KNOW WHAT THE CHANGES ARE!
THEN YOU SHOULD PROTEST THE "NEWS BLACKOUT." LET THE PUBLISHING COMPANY KNOW THAT YOU FEEL THE LOYAL FANS HAVE A RIGHT TO KNOW!
HMMM...LIS, I THINK I HAVE SOME WORK TO DO.
SEVERAL DAYS LATER, AT A CERTAIN COMIC BOOK PUBLISHING COMPANY...
EVERYONE, LET'S HAVE A BIG HAND FOR LINDSEY NAEGLE!

CONGRATULATIONS, LINDSEY!
YOU'VE GOT EVERYONE TALKING ABOUT RADIOACTIVE MAN AGAIN!
...WHAT ARE YOUR THOUGHTS ABOUT THE CHANGES IN THE U.S. BANKING SYSTEM, ALAN?
FRANKLY, BILL, I'M MORE CONCERNED ABOUT THE CHANGES THAT ARE PLANNED FOR RADIOACTIVE MAN. NO ONE HAS ANY IDEA WHAT'S IN STORE...
TODAY WE DISCUSS THE LORD'S GLORIOUS MYSTERIES, WHICH HAS NOTHING TO DO WITH THE GLORIOUS, YET MYSTERIOUS, NEW DIRECTION PLANNED FOR RADIOACTIVE MAN. GOD ONLY KNOWS WHAT THEY HAVE IN MIND!
...THIS LITTLE BABY IS AS GOOD AS NEW! SURE, MAYBE NOT AS NEW AS THE NEW RADIOACTIVE MAN, BUT PRETTY DARN CLOSE!

YOU'VE GOT EVERYONE WONDERING WHAT'S GONNA HAPPEN TO RADIOACTIVE MAN...
...AND THAT MEANS **SALES! SALES! SALES! WAH HA HA HA!**
UH, **BOSS?** JUST TO PLAY THE **DEVIL'S ADVOCATE--**
YEAH?
WELL, SIR, I WAS JUST LOOKING AT THE **PAGES** FOR THAT ISSUE...
...AND...WELL, UH...I JUST WONDER IF THE CUSTOMER WILL BE **SATISIFIED** WITH THIS APPROACH!

BWAH HA HA!
HA HA HA!
YOU'RE KIDDIN' ME, RIGHT? IT DOESN'T MATTER IF THE READER IS SATISFIED OR NOT, BUNKY!
IT'S THE SELLING OF THE COMIC THAT COUNTS!
WHETHER IT WORKS OR NOT IS A WHOLE OTHER THING! MY JOB IS TO MAKE SURE EVERY MAN, WOMAN AND FANBOY WANTS TO BUY A COPY OF "RADIOACTIVE MAN"!
AND AT THAT MOMENT, IN THE RECEPTION AREA...
:SIGH: LIKE I SAID, IF YOU DON'T HAVE AN APPOINTMENT, I CAN'T LET YOU IN. SORRY!
BUT IT IS IMPERATIVE THAT WE SEE THE PUBLISHER IMMEDIATELY!
WE HAVE A RIGHT TO KNOW WHAT'S BEING PLANNED FOR OUR HERO!
YEAH! WE HAVE A PETITION OF SIGNATURES FROM EVERYONE WHO WANTS TO KNOW!

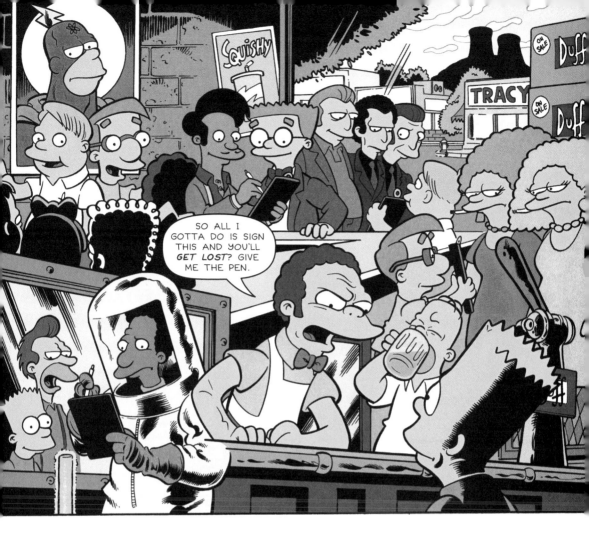

SO ALL I GOTTA DO IS SIGN THIS AND YOU'LL *GET LOST*? GIVE ME THE PEN.

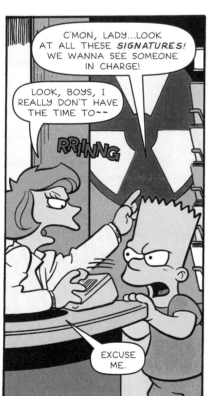

C'MON, LADY...LOOK AT ALL THESE *SIGNATURES*! WE WANNA SEE SOMEONE IN CHARGE!

LOOK, BOYS, I REALLY DON'T HAVE THE TIME TO--

RRINNG

EXCUSE ME.

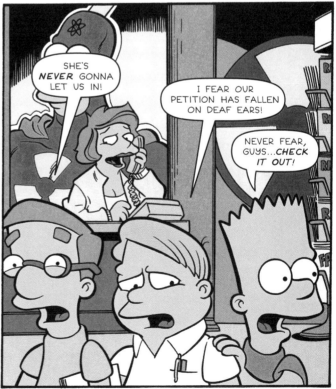

SHE'S *NEVER* GONNA LET US IN!

I FEAR OUR PETITION HAS FALLEN ON DEAF EARS!

NEVER FEAR, GUYS...*CHECK IT OUT*!

A LITTLE CELEBRATION IS IN ORDER, BOYS! LUNCH IS ON ME!
UP AND ATOM!
JUST DO ME A FAVOR... NO COMIC BOOK TALK WHILE WE'RE EATING! THERE'S ONLY SO MUCH I CAN TAKE DURING THE DAY!
YES, MS. NAEGLE!
HEY, GUYS, LOOK AT THIS!
IT IS A FEAST FOR OUR EYES, MY FRIENDS...DESPITE THE SENSORY OVERLOAD!
WHOA! SO THIS IS WHERE THE MAGIC HAPPENS!

OH WOW, IT LOOKS LIKE A NEW ITCHY & SCRATCHY COMIC!
LET'S GET A SNEAK PEEK!
BART, DO YOU THINK YOU OUGHT TO?
RELAX, MARTIN! I'M JUST GONNA SCROLL DOWN FOR A LOOK-SEE...
ITCHY AND SCRATCHY IN
THE LESION OF SUPER-HEROES
...AND WE WELCOME YOU, SCRATCHY, OUR NEWEST MEMBER!
CHOKE WHAT AN HONOR...
...TO BELONG TO A CLUB WHERE EACH MEMBER HAS AT LEAST ONE SUPER-POWER!
YES, ONE CAN SHOOT LIGHTNING BOLTS FROM HIS FINGER-TIPS, ONE CAN SPLIT IN TWO, ANOTHER CAN BECOME A GIANT.
AND ME?

I CAN CHANGE MY **FORM** AT WILL...
EEP!
...TO **ANY** SUPER-HERO I WANT!
SNIK!
SLASH!
SLASH!
SLASH!
WELCOME TO THE CLUB, **LESION-AIRE**!
CRASH!

I HOPE THEY ANIMATE THIS ONE SOMEDAY!
BWAH HA HA!
I SHARE YOUR AMUSEMENT, MY FRIENDS, BUT WE MUST. MAKE HASTE BEFORE SOMEONE COMES BACK
HOW THE HECK ARE WE GONNA FIND THE PUBLISHER?
ANYONE IN THAT POSITION WOULD CERTAINLY HAVE A CORNER OFFICE!
HOLD UP, GUYS...I WANNA HEAR THIS!
...SO I THOUGHT IT WOULD BE INTERESTING TO SHAKE UP THE SUPERIOR SQUAD LINE-UP!
THAT'S A GREAT IDEA!
AND HERE'S THE KICKER...
...WE REPLACE THE USUAL HEROES WITH SEVERAL CRUMMY CHARACTERS NO ONE CARES ABOUT!
GIMME A BREAK!
WHAT'S NOT TO LIKE ABOUT A BREAKDANCING SUPER-HERO?

EH?
YOU HEARD ME, MAN!
YOU'RE GONNA REPLACE THE WORLD'S GREATEST SUPER-HEROES WITH LOSERS?
WOW! WHO PUT YOU GUYS IN CHARGE?
WE BUY THE BOOK FOR REAL HEROES LIKE PLASMO, CAPTAIN SQUID, BUG BOY...
...AND OF COURSE, RADIOACTIVE MAN!
I LOOK FORWARD TO EVERY ISSUE JUST TO SEE LURE LASS!
I LIKE HOW SHE'S DRAWN, OKAY?
AHEM!

WHAT IS GOING ON HERE?! YOU GUYS ARE SUPPOSED TO BE IN A BRAIN-STORMING MEETING!
HE DIDN'T KEEP THE DOOR CLOSED!
KRUSTY! YOU'RE THE GUY WE NEED TO TALK TO!
WE'VE BEEN READING RADIOACTIVE MAN COMICS FOR AS LONG AS WE CAN REMEMBER!
AS THE NEW PUBLISHER, SIR, YOU'D PROBABLY WANT TO HEAR WHAT YOUR READERS THINK.
NOT REALLY.
BUT KRUSTY, WE GOT ALMOST EVERYONE IN SPRINGFIELD TO SIGN THIS PETITION.
FROM YOUNG CHILDREN TO SENIOR CITIZENS, THEY HAD ONE THING IN COMMON...
...THEIR LOVE FOR RADIOACTIVE MAN!
PETITION
WE GOT TONS OF SIGNATURES OF PEOPLE FROM ALL OVER TOWN WHO WANT TO KNOW WHAT YOU HAVE PLANNED FOR THEIR HERO.
THEY SIGNED BECAUSE THEY WANT TO KNOW IF THE CHANGES WILL BE GOOD CHANGES.
MORE IMPORTANTLY, THEY SIGNED BECAUSE THEY CARED!

YOU MEAN, YOU BOYS WENT THROUGH ALL THIS TROUBLE FOR A COMIC BOOK CHARACTER?
NOT JUST ANY COMIC BOOK CHARACTER, KRUSTY...
...WE DID IT FOR RADIOACTIVE MAN!
BOYS, I MAY BE NEW TO THE COMIC BOOK BUSINESS, BUT I HAVE LEARNED SOMETHING TODAY...
...I LEARNED THAT RADIOACTIVE MAN'S LOYAL READERS WILL GO THROUGH GREAT LENGTHS FOR THEIR FAVORITE CHARACTER.
I THANK YOU FOR YOUR DEDICATION AND THE COMPANY WOULD LIKE TO THANK YOU WITH TOKENS OF OUR APPRECIATION.
FIND SOME TCHOTCHKES FOR THESE BRATS AND SHOW 'EM THE DOOR!

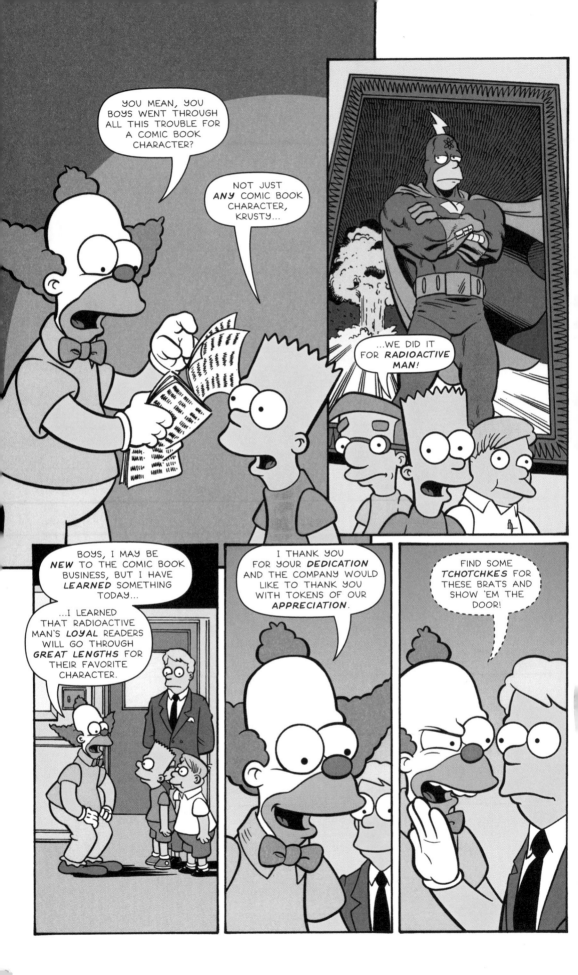

AND SO...
MISSION ACCOMPLISHED!
I'LL SAY!
YOU BET!
NOT ONLY DID WE MAKE A DIFFERENCE, BUT WE WALKED AWAY WITH SOME SWAG!
I CAN'T WAIT TO SEE WHAT I CAN GET FOR SOME OF THIS STUFF ON EBUY!
IT'S ALL GOOD, MEN!
COME WHAT MAY, WE CAN SLEEP EASY TONIGHT.
PETITIO
"WE KNOW THAT OUR CONCERNS HAVE BEEN HEARD AND OUR PETITION HAS BEEN PUT IN THE PROPER HANDS."
"TRULY, THE PEOPLE HAVE SPOKEN!"

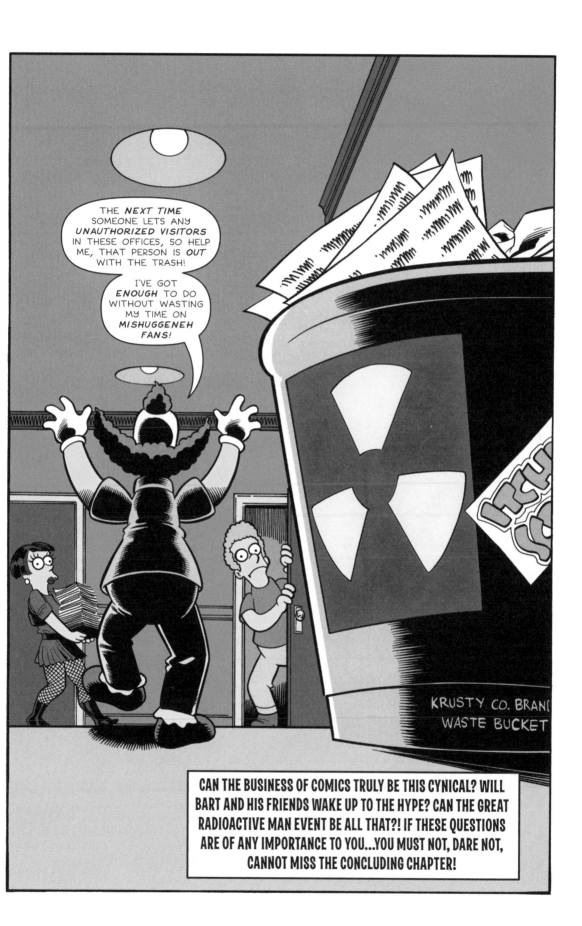

CAN THE BUSINESS OF COMICS TRULY BE THIS CYNICAL? WILL BART AND HIS FRIENDS WAKE UP TO THE HYPE? CAN THE GREAT RADIOACTIVE MAN EVENT BE ALL THAT?! IF THESE QUESTIONS ARE OF ANY IMPORTANCE TO YOU...YOU MUST NOT, DARE NOT, CANNOT MISS THE CONCLUDING CHAPTER!

AD SPACE
Samsons
WHERE IN THE WORLD IS RADIOACTIVE MAN??
73

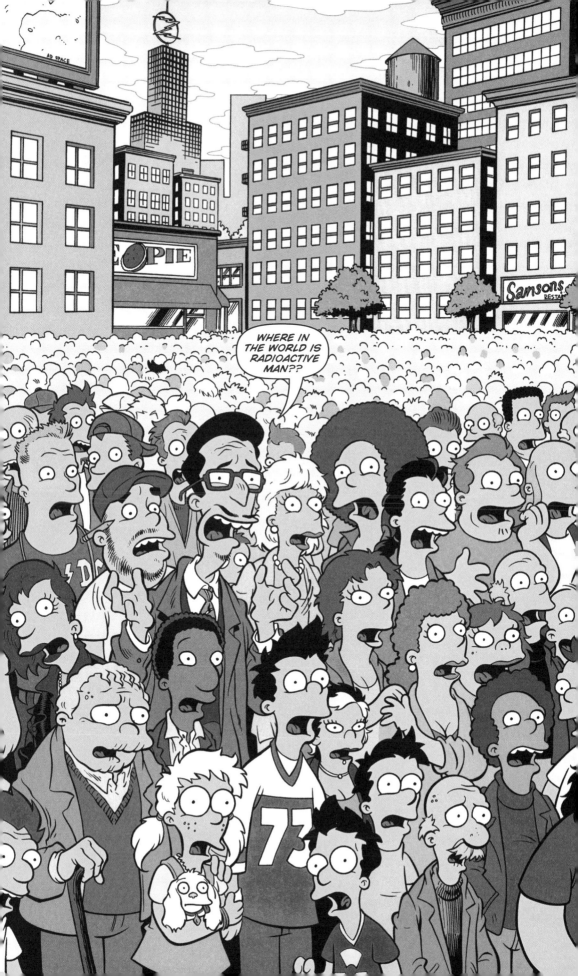

DON'T WORRY?! RADIOACTIVE MAN HASN'T BEEN SEEN IN WEEKS!
PLEASE, CITIZENS OF ZENITH...DON'T WORRY!
DISASTERS ARE EVERYWHERE!
WHO'S GONNA SAVE US...
CRIME IS OUT OF CONTROL!
WE'RE NOT USED TO HELPING OURSELVES!
YEAH!
EVERYONE... GET A GRIP!
RADIOACTIVE MAN WILL BE BACK ...I HOPE!
FALLOUT BOY! HEY! OVER HERE!
I KEEP TRYING TO GET HIS ATTENTION, BUT IT'S NO USE!
IN FACT, I TRY TO GET ANYONE'S ATTENTION, AND IT PROVES FUTILE...
HELLO?
YOO HOO!
HAS RADIOACTIVE MAN'S ARCH FOE GOTTEN THE BEST OF HIM AT LAST?!
HERE I AM!
YO!
HEY! ANYBODY?!
IS THE IRRADIATED CRUSADER DOOMED TO SPEND ETERNITY IN...THE OBLIVIOUS ZONE?!

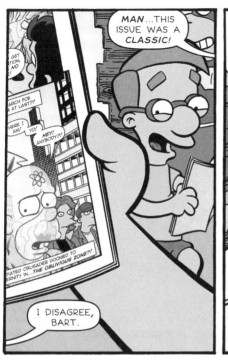

MAN...THIS ISSUE WAS A *CLASSIC!*

I DISAGREE, BART.

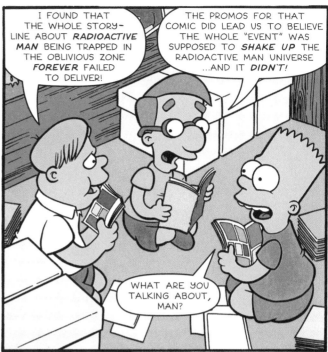

I FOUND THAT THE WHOLE STORY-LINE ABOUT *RADIOACTIVE MAN* BEING TRAPPED IN THE OBLIVIOUS ZONE *FOREVER* FAILED TO DELIVER!

THE PROMOS FOR THAT COMIC DID LEAD US TO BELIEVE THE WHOLE "EVENT" WAS SUPPOSED TO *SHAKE UP* THE RADIOACTIVE MAN UNIVERSE ...AND IT *DIDN'T!*

WHAT ARE YOU TALKING ABOUT, MAN?

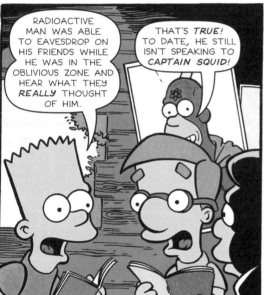

RADIOACTIVE MAN WAS ABLE TO EAVESDROP ON HIS FRIENDS WHILE HE WAS IN THE OBLIVIOUS ZONE AND HEAR WHAT THEY *REALLY* THOUGHT OF HIM.

THAT'S *TRUE!* TO DATE, HE STILL ISN'T SPEAKING TO *CAPTAIN SQUID!*

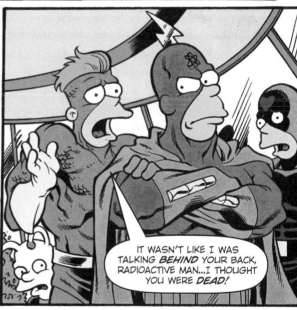

IT WASN'T LIKE I WAS TALKING *BEHIND* YOUR BACK, RADIOACTIVE MAN...I THOUGHT YOU WERE *DEAD!*

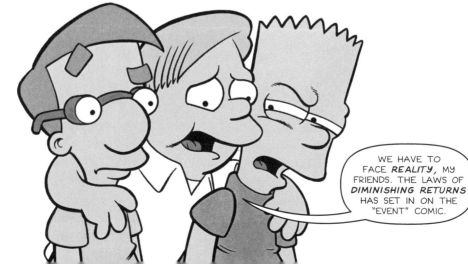

WE HAVE TO FACE *REALITY,* MY FRIENDS. THE LAWS OF *DIMINISHING RETURNS* HAS SET IN ON THE "EVENT" COMIC.

"WHETHER RADIOACTIVE MAN IS CAST INTO THE OBLIVIOUS ZONE..."
SEE ME...? HEAR ME...? FEEL ME...?
"...OR BUG BOY'S PEOPLE COME TO EARTH TO TAKE HIM HOME..."
SOMETHING TELLS ME BUG BOY LIKES IT BETTER HERE!
"...OR BRAVE HEART'S LONG-BELIEVED-DEAD FATHER RETURNS TO KILL HIS SON..."
DAD...?!
HELLO, SON...
... AND GOODBYE!
BANG!
AND AFTER WEEKS OF WONDERING, WORRYING, AND WAITING TO SEE WHAT CHANGES WILL BE MADE TO RADIOACTIVE MAN...
WELL, THE NEW RADIOACTIVE MAN COMIC HITS THE STANDS TODAY!
...THE "EVENT" CAN'T LIVE UP TO THE HYPE!

THE BEST RADIOACTIVE MAN EVENT EVER!
PART 3
...IT BETTER DELIVER!
MATT GROENING
BATTON LASH SCRIPT
TONE RODRIGUEZ PENCILS
ANDREW PEPOY INKS
ART VILLANUEVA COLORS
KAREN BATES LETTERS
BILL MORRISON EDITOR

HERE'S TO LINDSEY NAEGLE, FOR BEING RESPONSIBLE FOR THE HIGHEST-ORDERED ISSUE OF "RADIOACTIVE MAN" IN THE TITLE'S HISTORY!
SALES AND MARKETING HAVE NEVER DONE BETTER SINCE YOU CAME ABOARD, LINDSEY!
JUST DOING MY JOB, CHIEF!
HERE, HERE!
I HAVE A FEELING YOU'RE GOING PLACES IN THIS COMPANY, LINDSEY!
I CERTAINLY HOPE SO, CHIEF!
HMM! THE RADIOACTIVE MAN COMIC REMAINS HOT, BUT THIS COFFEE IS TEPID AT BEST!
I'M ON IT, CHIEF!
THE BOSS!

I CERTAINLY HOPE SO, KRUSTY...I MEAN, CHIEF!
THE NEW RADIOACTIVE MAN MUST BE DRIVING THE FANBOYS CRAZY! THEY DON'T KNOW WHAT TO EXPECT!
SERVES 'EM RIGHT! THOSE GEEKS WANT US TO DO SOMETHING NEW, BUT THEY NEVER REALLY WANT ANYTHING TO CHANGE! EVEN WHEN WE TRY TO LET THEM HAVE IT BOTH WAYS...
IT WAS THE CROSSOVER EVENT YOU WERE WAITING FOR WHEN TWO WORLDS COLLIDED!
Y-YOU MEAN YOU DON'T LIKE THE WAY IT IS TODAY...?
YOU GOTTA BE KIDDING, RADIOACTIVE MAN! THE WORLD WAS MUCH BETTER WHERE I CAME FROM!
BUT IN YOUR DAY, RADIO MAN, THERE WAS A WORLD WAR...NO PENICILLIN... BAD INDOOR PLUMBING!
YES, BUT LOOK AT YOUR ERA...WEAPONS OF MASS DESTRUCTION... GLOBAL FINANCIAL CRISIS... "MEET THE KARDASHIANS"!
TAKE THAT BACK!
MAKE ME!
I'M TIRED OF HEARING ABOUT "THE GOOD OLD DAYS"...
...YOU'LL COME TO SEE THAT THE 31ST CENTURY IS THE BEST!
JUMPIN' JEEPERS! IT'S THE RADIOACTIVE MAN FROM THE FUTURE!
SIZZLIN' SHORT-WAVES!

I MEAN, REALLY! WHO COULD BE POSSIBLY CARE THAT MUCH?
I WAS SO LOOKING FORWARD TO THAT TEAM-UP...
...THREE HEROES FROM THREE ERAS! HOW COULD IT MISS? BORING!
IT DIDN'T HELP THAT FIGHTING WAS OBSOLETE BY THE 31ST CENTURY!
YOU WON'T GET AWAY WITH YOUR EVIL PLAN, X-K95!
YOU AND YOUR COUNTERPARTS WILL NEVER STOP ME!
GOOD THOUGHTS VS. BAD THOUGHTS? SHEESH!
WHEN IN ROME, RADIO MAN...
I'D RATHER SEE THE HEROES KICK BUTT THAN DEAL WITH EXISTENTIAL ANGST!
THE SCIENCE WAS ALL OVER THE PLACE, BUT YOU HAVE TO ADMIT THE RADIOACTIVE MAN OF THE FUTURE LOOKED AWESOME!
YEAH, BUT IT TOOK TEN ISSUES, TWENTY CROSSOVERS, AND THREE SPECIALS TO READ SOMETHING THAT COULD'VE BEEN TOLD IN ONE ISSUE!
I WISH THAT WAS THE CASE! I CAN'T AFFORD A WHOLE "EVENT" STORYLINE!
NO ARGUMENT THERE, MY FRIENDS...

...MAYBE THIS LATEST "EVENT" COMIC WILL PLEASANTLY SURPRISE US!
THE COMIC BOOK GUY SAYS THERE'S A LIMIT ON HOW MANY COPIES WE CAN BUY!
YEAH...ONLY 20 COPIES PER CUSTOMER? IT AIN'T FAIR, I TELL YOU!
GEE, MRS. KRABAPPEL, ARE YOU A RADIO-ACTIVE MAN FAN?
NO, BUT IN THIS RECESSION, THAT COMIC BOOK MAY BE MORE RELIABLE FOR MY RETIREMENT THAN MY 401K!
YOU MEAN THIS ISN'T THE DMV?
NOW, IN MY DAY, FUNNY BOOKS WERE ONLY A PENNY, AND THE NEWSSTAND WOULD GIVE OUT A SET A DISHES WHEN WE BOUGHT ONE. I WISH I'D SAVED THOSE DISHES...THEY'D BE WORTH A FORTUNE TODAY!

I'VE BEEN ON THIS LINE FOR HOURS!
ME, TOO! WHEN CAN WE BUY THE COMIC ALREADY?
DON'T LOOK NOW...

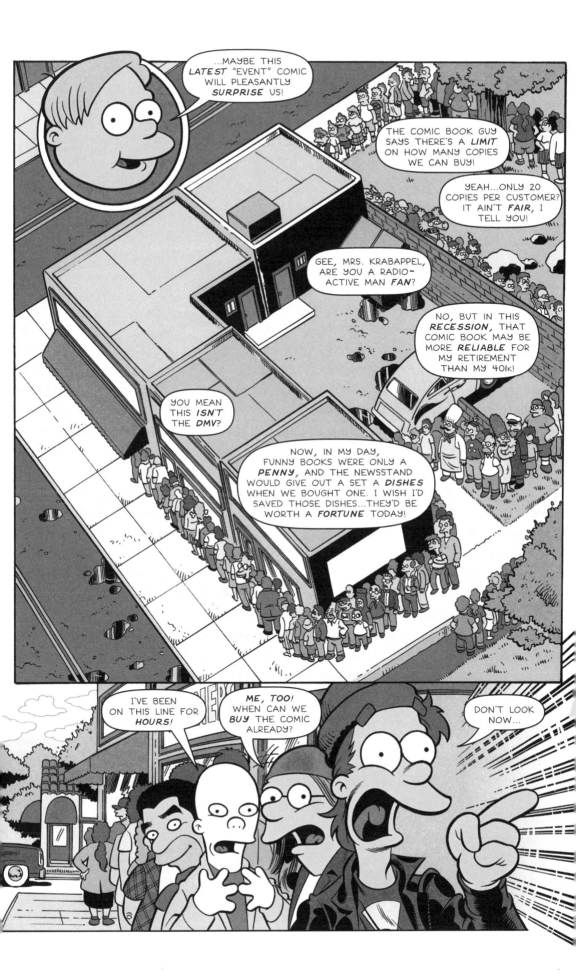

...BUT I THINK THE STORE'S COPIES ARE *ARRIVING!*
S DUNGEON CARD SHOP
CLEANE
FRANK'S PRINT
UP EXPRESS
14 BO
ONE SIDE! ONE SIDE! LET HIM THROUGH!
NEW RADIOACTIVE MAN
:GRUNT!: THESE "EVENT COMICS" ARE GONNA *KILL* ME!
PEOPLE, *PLEASE*. I KNOW YOU HAVE *ANTICIPATED* THIS MOMENT FOR *WEEKS*. HOWEVER...
...I HAVE ONLY BEEN *ALLOCATED* A CERTAIN NUMBER OF COPIES. SO IT WILL BE FIRST COME...
NEW
...FIRST SERVED!
RADIOACTIVE MAN
RADIOACTIVE MAN
WHOOM!

FOR A MINUTE THERE, I THOUGHT IT WAS GOING TO BE SOLD OUT!
LUCKILY, WE MANAGED TO PROCURE COPIES!
I DON'T KNOW ABOUT YOU GUYS...
...BUT I'M GOING TO PULL UP A CURB AND CHECK THIS PUPPY OUT!
GOOD IDEA! I'M TOO CURIOUS TO WAIT TO GET HOME TO READ IT!
YEAH...LET'S SEE EXACTLY WHAT THIS "BOLD NEW DIRECTION FOR RADIOACTIVE MAN IS ALL ABOUT!
LET ME SEE YOUR COPY.
I THOUGHT THERE WAS SOMETHING WRONG WITH MY GLASSES, BUT I GUESS NOT!
MAYBE IT'S A PRINTING ERROR...?
IT'S NO MISTAKE, GUYS... THIS WAS INTENTIONAL!

I CAN'T BELIEVE IT WAS SOLD OUT SO QUICKLY!
I TOLD YOU WE SHOULD'VE CAMPED OUT LAST NIGHT!
HEY, KID...SO WHAT'S THE BIG CHANGE IN RADIO-ACTIVE MAN?
NOTHING.
AFTER ALL THAT HYPE?
SO WHAT'S THE NEW APPROACH, THEN?
LIKE HE SAID... NOTHING!
CHECK IT OUT...
MAN, THEY'VE GOT TO BE KIDDING!

WE'RE **NOT** KIDDING!
FANS ARE ALWAYS **COMPLAINING** WHENEVER WE COMIC BOOK PUBLISHERS TRY SOMETHING NEW! **NOTHING** WE DO SEEMS TO LIVE UP TO FANS' **PRECONCEIVED NOTIONS**!
WITH THAT IN MIND, WE DECIDED TO LET **EACH** READER BE RESPONSIBLE FOR WHAT THEY WANT TO READ! **NO LONGER** DO THOSE GEEKS HAVE TO BE **UPSET** WITH THE WAY WE HANDLE THEIR FAVORITE CHARACTERS!
LOOK HERE...YOU GET A **LOGO, RULED PANELS,** EMPTY **WORD BALLONS,** AND WE THROW IN **NUMBERED PAGES,** TOO!
NOW THE **READER** CAN JUST GRAB A PENCIL AND DO THE COMIC IN **ANY** DIRECTION HE OR SHE WISHES! IT'S **WIN-WIN,** I THINK!
DO YOU **REALLY** THINK THIS IS GOING TO FLY WITH YOUR READERSHIP?
WHADDAYA KIDDIN'? THIS HAS BEEN THE HIGHEST-SELLING ISSUE OF RADIOACTIVE MAN...**EVER**!
PRESS

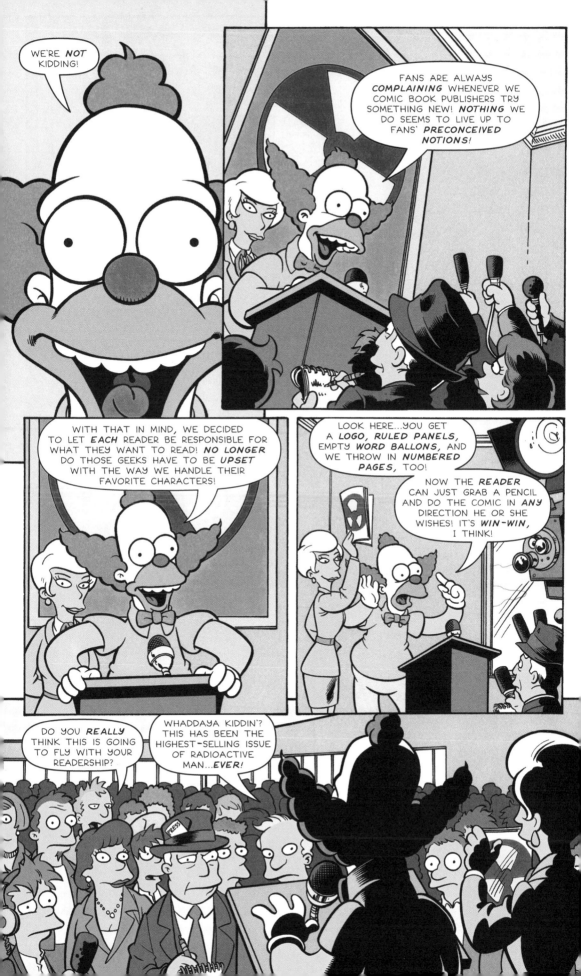

WE PROMISED A BIG CHANGE...AND NO ONE CAN DENY THAT THIS IS A BIG CHANGE! WA-HOO-HOO-HEY!
GROAN!
I BUY COMICS TO BE ENTERTAINED, NOT TO DO THE ENTERTAINING! THIS IDEA BLOWS!
BUT THIS IS A GREAT IDEA, BART! I ALWAYS HAD PROBLEMS TRYING TO FOLLOW WORDS AND PICTURES, BUT NOT ANYMORE!
I SURE MISS THE OLD "RADIOACTIVE MAN". I DON'T NEED AN EVENT...JUST A GOOD STORY!
WELL, YOU CAN SEND A MESSAGE TO THE PUBLISHER TELLING THEM JUST THAT, BART.
AW...THEY NEVER LISTEN TO THE FANS, LIS!
BUT YOU CAN SHOW THEM HOW IT SHOULD DONE, BART... AND IN THEIR VERY OWN PUBLICATION!
AH-HA!

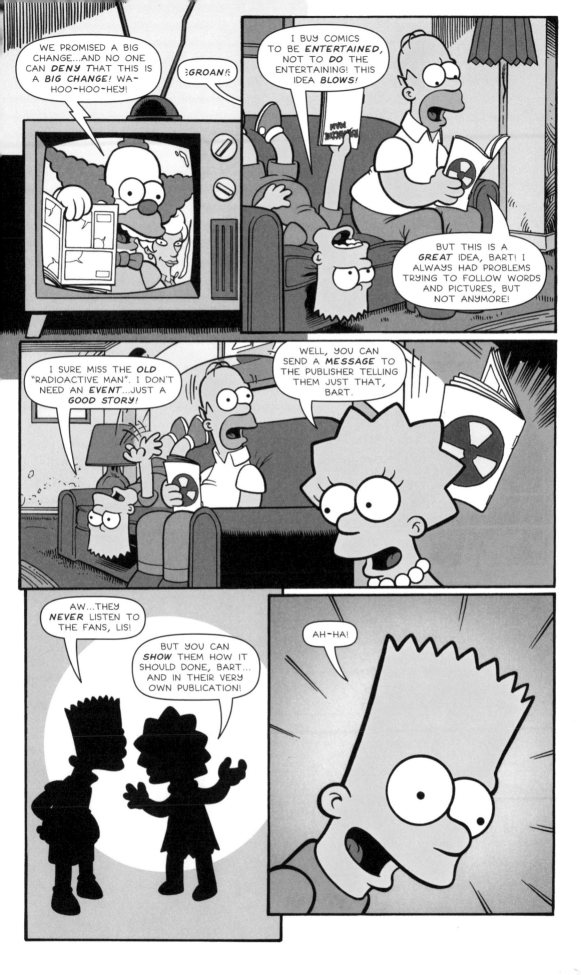

SEVERAL WEEKS LATER...
SO! THE HEAD CLOWN WANTS TO SEE ME!
KRUSTY'S FINALLY COME AROUND TO THAT RAISE...
...OR MAYBE THAT CORNER OFFICE! WHATEVER. THIS IS JUST THE BEGINNING!
I'M WHAT?!
YOU HEARD ME, NAEGLE...FIRED!
BUT-BUT...WHY?

HERE'S THE SALES REPORT FOR THE **FIRST** ISSUE OF THE **RADICAL NEW APPROACH** TO "RADIOACTIVE MAN"...THROUGH THE **ROOF!**
NOW HERE ARE THE ORDERS FOR THE **SECOND** ISSUE...IN THE **BASEMENT!**
WELL, CHIEF, YOU HAVE TO TAKE INTO CONSIDERATION THAT THERE WILL BE...**PEAKS** AND **VALLEYS** IN PUBLISHING AND--
STOW IT, SISTER! YOUR "DO-IT-YOURSELF" CONCEPT HAS YIELDED THIS **MASTERPIECE!**
?
RADIOACTIVE MAN VS THE BIG FAT NOTHING
By Bart Simpson
JEEPERS! WHAT IS THIS **BIG FAT NOTHING** DOING TO PEOPLE??

RADIOACTIVE MAN! YOU'VE GOT TO HELP US! EVERYONE'S FALLEN UNDER THE SPELL OF THIS BIG FAT NOTHING!
WOW...
AWESOME...
GREAT...
THE BIG FAT NOTHING IS COMIN
YOUR NOBODY IF YOU DON'T GET WITH THE
DONT DARE MISS THE BIG FAT NOTHING
EVERYONE'S BEING TOLD A LIE! THEY THINK THEY'RE GETTING SOME-THING, BUT ALL THEY'RE GETTING IS...
BFN
BIG FAT
...A BIG, FAT, NOTHING?
I'M NOT SURE I CAN DO ANYTHING, SON! IF PEOPLE WANT TO GO WITH A BIG FAT NOTHING, I CAN'T STOP THEM!
BUT IF YOU COME WITH ME, WE'LL JOIN THE SUPERIOR SQUAD IN SOME REAL MINDLESS, HEART-STOPPING ACTION!
COOL!

GO, GUYS, GO!
THE KID DRAWS ALL HIS FAVORITE HEROES IN FIGHTS WITH TONS OF GORE...SO WHAT?

TCH!! IF YOU ASK ME, THE BRAT WHO DID THIS IS CRAVING ATTENTION BY SENDING IT TO YOU, CHIEF!
HE DIDN'T SEND IT TO ME ORIGINALLY...THAT'S A COPY OF THE ONE HE SENT TO KENT BROCKMAN!
BART SIMPSON'S RADIOACTIVE MAN
BROCKMAN'S STAFF SENT IT TO ME TO GET MY REACTION! LOOK!
AH...MUST BE A SLOW NEWS DAY!
...AND HAS LIFTED SANCTIONS ON CUBA. BUT IN OUR TOP STORY TONIGHT...
BIG FAT NOTHING
...ONE YOUNG FAN DECIDED TO MAKE LEMONADE OUT OF LEMONS AFTER THE BITTER DISAPPOINTMENT OF THE "BOLD NEW DIRECTION" FOR HIS FAVORITE COMIC BOOK CHARACTER, THANKS TO A VERY LAZY PUBLISHER...
BART SIMPSON'S RADIOACTIVE MAN
"...BUT INSTEAD OF A LEMONADE STAND, RESOURCEFUL BART SIMPSON MADE COPIES OF THE STORY HE CREATED IN THE BLANK PAGES OF THE NEW RADIOACTIVE MAN COMIC AND IS SELLING THEM FOR HIS OWN PROFIT!"
HOW DO YOU LIKE YOUR FRIEND'S VERSION OF "RADIOACTIVE MAN"?
BART PUTS EVERYTHING I ALWAYS WANTED TO SEE IN A RADIOACTIVE MAN STORY!
YEAH! LIMBS FLYING, BLOOD SPLATTERING, GORE ALL OVER THE PLACE!
FINALLY! A COMIC WITH SOME SUBSTANCE!

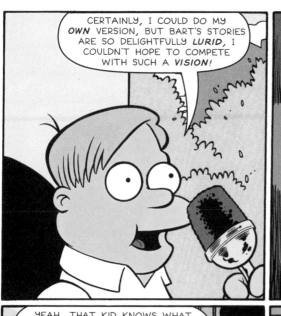

CERTAINLY, I COULD DO MY *OWN* VERSION, BUT BART'S STORIES ARE SO DELIGHTFULLY *LURID*, I COULDN'T HOPE TO COMPETE WITH SUCH A *VISION!*

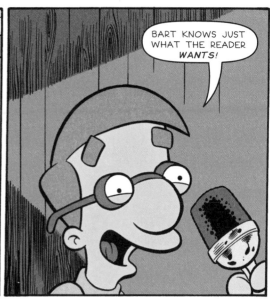

BART KNOWS JUST WHAT THE READER *WANTS!*

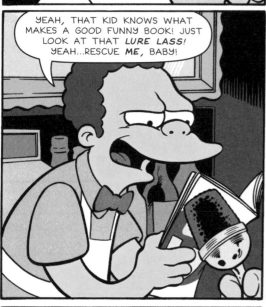

YEAH, THAT KID KNOWS WHAT MAKES A GOOD FUNNY BOOK! JUST LOOK AT THAT *LURE LASS!* YEAH...RESCUE *ME,* BABY!

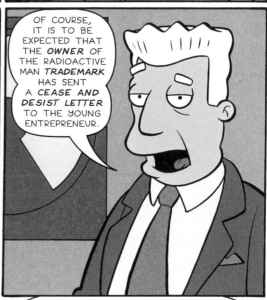

OF COURSE, IT IS TO BE EXPECTED THAT THE *OWNER* OF THE *RADIOACTIVE MAN* TRADEMARK HAS SENT A *CEASE AND DESIST LETTER* TO THE YOUNG ENTREPRENEUR.

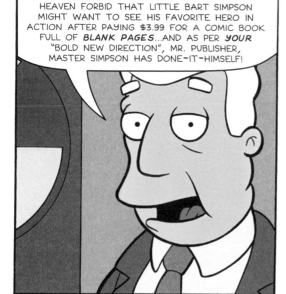

HEAVEN FORBID THAT LITTLE BART SIMPSON MIGHT WANT TO SEE HIS FAVORITE HERO IN ACTION AFTER PAYING $3.99 FOR A COMIC BOOK FULL OF *BLANK PAGES*...AND AS PER *YOUR* "BOLD NEW DIRECTION", MR. PUBLISHER, MASTER SIMPSON HAS DONE-IT-HIMSELF!

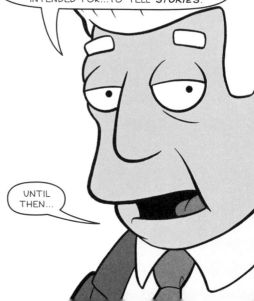

I SUGGEST TO YOU, SIR, THAT INSTEAD OF STAGING TIRESOME "EVENTS" THAT SEND MIXED MESSAGES, YOU SHOULD USE YOUR PUBLICATION FOR WHAT IT WAS ORIGINALLY INTENDED FOR...TO TELL *STORIES*.

UNTIL THEN...

"...YOU, KRUSTY THE CLOWN, ARE THE CRUMMIEST PERSON IN THE UNIVERSE!"
CRUMMIEST
YOU KNOW, CHIEF... THERE ARE MUCH WORSE PEOPLE IN THE UNIV--
GET OUT!!!
SECURITY WILL SEE YOU OUT, NAEGLE!
HAW HAW!

AND WILL SOMEBODY GET A COUPLE OF CREATIVE PEOPLE ON THE HORN? WE'VE GOT A COMIC BOOK TO PRODUCE!
THE ANDROID'S DUNGEON & BASEBALL CARD SHOP
SEVERAL MONTHS LATER...
HEY, COMIC BOOK GUY, HAS THE NEW ISSUE OF "RADIOACTIVE MAN" ARRIVED?
SIGH YOU SHOULD KNOW BY NOW, IT IS RACKED IN THE "NEW ARRIVALS" SECTION IN ALPHABETICAL ORDER...
...IF YOU DO NOT SEE IT, IT MEANS IT HAS SOLD OUT, THOUGH I DOUBT IT!
AH! HERE IT IS!
JOSS
RADIOACTIVE MAN
14 BOLT!
CAPTAIN SQUID
HOBO COMIX
IT IS GOOD TO SEE THE COMIC GOING BACK TO BASICS!
FINALLY! THOSE "EVENTS" WERE WEARING ME OUT!
I'M GLAD KRUSTY SAW THE LIGHT AND HIRED A CREATIVE TEAM THAT JUST WANTS TO TELL STORIES!
I STILL SAY THEY SHOULD'VE HIRED YOU, BART!
YES! YOUR RADIOACTIVE MAN COMICS AT LEAST KEPT TRUE TO THE SPIRIT OF THE FEATURE!
THANKS, GUYS...BUT IT TAKES A LONG TIME TO DO A COMIC BOOK! THE MONEY I GOT FOR IT WASN'T REALLY WORTH MY TIME!

ANYWAY, I THINK MY CALLING IS READING COMICS! I'LL LEAVE CREATING TO THE PROFESSIONALS!
BUT IT WAS YOUR EFFORT THAT SHAMED THE COMPANY INTO GETTING THEIR ACT TOGETHER!
LOOK, BART! YOU'RE IN THE COMIC!
ROBOT MAN
SANZ PANTZ
AIR SPACE
MY DAD COMICS
CAPTAIN SQUID
CRAZY COMICS
U.T.F.
JO$$ COMICS
CAPS MONTHLY
NM
THIS MUST BE THE CREATIVE TEAM'S WAY OF THANKING YOU!
A ROYALTY CHECK WOULD'VE BEEN NICE, BUT STILL...
NO, IT'S MAYHEM!
THE DOCTOR SAYS MY FOOT WILL BE IN CAST FOR AT LEAST SIX WEEKS!
I'M HAPPY TO DO MY PART IN HELPING THE GREATEST SUPER-HERO EVER!

THAT'S THE LAST TIME I KICK A TITANIUM-PLATED ROBOT!
DON'T WORRY, FALLOUT BOY! RADIOACTIVE MAN IS WORKING WITH A TEMPORARY SIDEKICK UNTIL YOU GET BETTER!
PLEASE DON'T TELL ME IT'S A WANNABE LIKE GLOW BOY OR NUCLEAR LAD!
RELAX, FALLOUT BOY! RADIOACTIVE MAN KNOWS BETTER THAN THAT!
HE FOUND SOMEONE HE CAN COUNT ON...
THANKS FOR HELPING ME OUT, BART! I KNEW I COULD RELY ON YOU!
NO PROBLEMO, RADIOACTIVE MAN! I'M HERE FOR YOU!
THEN WHAT ARE WE WAITING FOR? UP AND ATOM!
LET'S GO KICK SOME SUPER-VILLAIN BUTT, DUDE!

COOL! I CAN'T WAIT TO READ THIS!
RADIOACTIVE MAN
NOT AN EVENT! JUST A GOOD, OLD-FASHIONED STORY!
CHUCKLE THOSE KIDS REMIND ME OF WHEN I WAS THEIR AGE... WHEN I COULDN'T WAIT TO READ THE NEWEST ISSUES OF MY FAVORITE COMICS!
HMM...
SUPERIOR SQUAD
RADIOACTIVE MAN
RADIOACTIVE MAN
SUPERIOR SQUAD
RADIOACTIVE MAN SPECIAL
U.T.F.
ACTUALLY READ THE COMICS? I GUESS ONE COULD IF ONE IS SO INCLINED!
AND SO IT GOES...FOR NOW.
THE END!

LI'L HOMER in MEAN GENIE

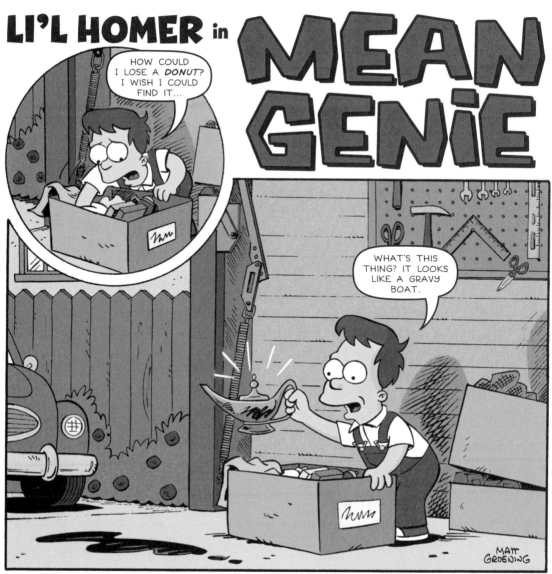

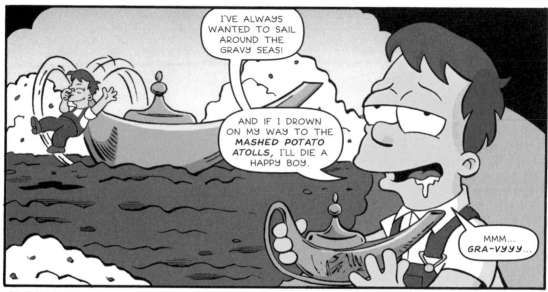

CAROL LAY
STORY & ART

NATHAN HAMILL
COLORS

KAREN BATES
LETTERS

NATHAN KANE
EDITOR

WHAT'S THIS SCRATCHED ON THE SIDE?
I HOPE IT'S A MAP TO THE GRAVY SEA!
RUB
RUB
UH-OH...
WHAT TH--?!
JIMINY CRICKET! WHO THE HECK ARE YOU?
I AM YOUR SERVANT FOR AS LONG AS YOU POSSESS THE LAMP.
MY SERVANT? YOU MEAN YOU'LL DO WHATEVER I ASK?
YYY-YESS-SSSSS...
POOF!

IF YOU SHOULD GIVE AWAY OR LOSE THE LAMP, HOWEVER, I WILL **DESTROY** YOU.
WHAT?!
I HAVE ABANDONMENT ISSUES.
I THOUGHT GENIES GRANT THREE WISHES AND THEN GO AWAY! NOBODY EVER SAID ANYTHING ABOUT **KILLING** ANYBODY!
THAT'S JUST A ***FAIRY TALE***.
PIFF!
ALLOW ME TO SPELL IT OUT FOR YOU.
"THE PENALTY FOR LOSING OR GIVING AWAY THE LAMP IS **DEATH**."
BUT ALL I **DO** IS LOSE THINGS! I CAN'T EVEN FIND MY ***DONUT!***
"FURTHERMORE, I AM NOT LIABLE FOR ANY WISHES YOU MAKE THAT MAY RESULT IN THE EXTERMINATION OF YOUR LOVED ONES OR OTHERS."
GASP!
WHAT DO YOU MEAN?!

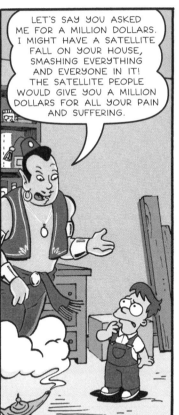

LET'S SAY YOU ASKED ME FOR A MILLION DOLLARS. I MIGHT HAVE A SATELLITE FALL ON YOUR HOUSE, SMASHING EVERYTHING AND EVERYONE IN IT! THE SATELLITE PEOPLE WOULD GIVE YOU A MILLION DOLLARS FOR ALL YOUR PAIN AND SUFFERING.

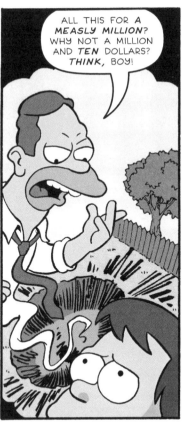

ALL THIS FOR *A MEASLY MILLION*? WHY NOT A MILLION AND *TEN* DOLLARS? *THINK*, BOY!

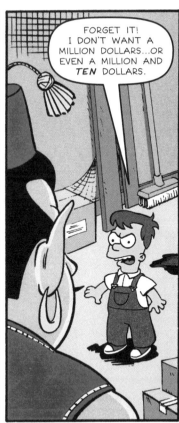

FORGET IT! I DON'T WANT A MILLION DOLLARS...OR EVEN A MILLION AND *TEN* DOLLARS.

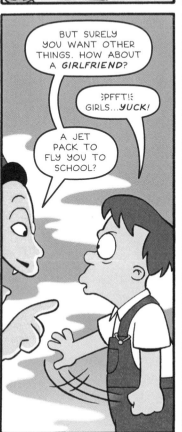

BUT SURELY YOU WANT OTHER THINGS. HOW ABOUT A *GIRLFRIEND*?

⋮PFFT!⋮ GIRLS...*YUCK!*

A JET PACK TO FLY YOU TO SCHOOL?

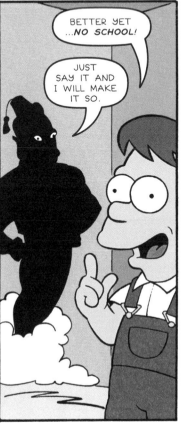

BETTER YET ...*NO SCHOOL!*

JUST SAY IT AND I WILL MAKE IT SO.

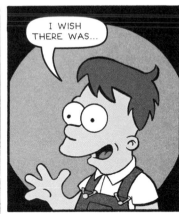

I WISH THERE WAS...

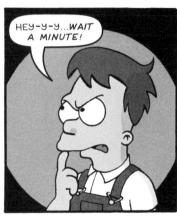

HEY-Y-Y...*WAIT A MINUTE!*

WHAT IF YOU SHUT DOWN THE SCHOOL BY MAKING A VOLCANO ERUPT, AND IT KILLS ALL MY FRIENDS AND TEACHERS??
THAT MIGHT MAKE ME **FEEL** BAD.
HEY! WHO'S THIS GUY, AND WHY'S HE WEARING MY CABAÑA ENSEMBLE?
HE'S A **MEAN GENIE**, DAD. HE WANTS ME TO MAKE **WISHES** THAT CAN HURT PEOPLE.
WHAT CAN I DO?
YEP, THIS ONE'S AN OLD **TRICKSTER**, ALL RIGHT. YOU CAN TELL BY THE CROSSED SCIMITARS.
ANY WISH YOU MAKE IS GOING TO HURT **SOMEONE** SOMEWHERE.
GOOD LUCK WITH THAT, KID.
DAD! WAIT!
IF YOU HELP ME, I CAN WISH FOR YOU TO HAVE A NEW **WIFE**.
I SURE COULD USE A **MOM**.
AND **I** COULD USE A CHIEF COOK AND BOTTLE WASHER.
OKAY, WHAT DO YOU GOT?
I CAN WISH TO BECOME THE BEST **YO-YO CHAMPION IN THE WORLD!**
SURE, THAT **SOUNDS** HARMLESS, BUT THIS CHARACTER IS TRICKY.
BUT I'M ALREADY PRETTY GOOD, SO NO ONE HAS TO GET HURT.

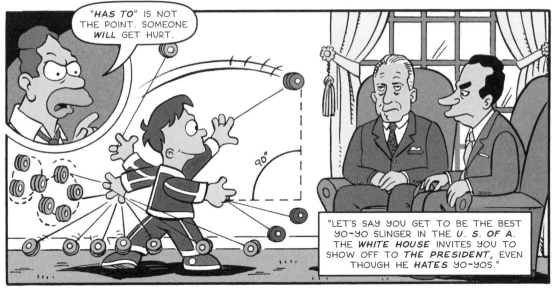

"HAS TO" IS NOT THE POINT. SOMEONE **WILL** GET HURT.

90°

"LET'S SAY YOU GET TO BE THE BEST YO-YO SLINGER IN THE *U. S. OF A.* THE *WHITE HOUSE* INVITES YOU TO SHOW OFF TO *THE PRESIDENT,* EVEN THOUGH HE *HATES* YO-YOS."

"THE YO-YO BREAKS OUT OF ITS ORBIT AND FLIES STRAIGHT UP NIXON'S NOSE, PIERCING HIS BRAIN AND KILLING HIM INSTANTLY."

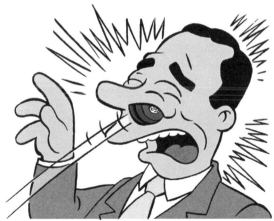

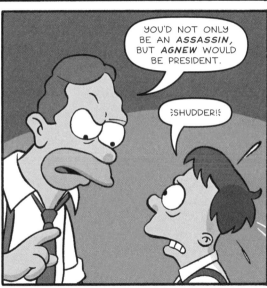

YOU'D NOT ONLY BE AN *ASSASSIN,* BUT *AGNEW* WOULD BE PRESIDENT.

:SHUDDER!:

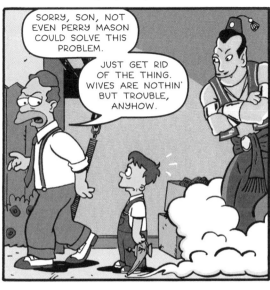

SORRY, SON, NOT EVEN PERRY MASON COULD SOLVE THIS PROBLEM.

JUST GET RID OF THE THING. WIVES ARE NOTHIN' BUT TROUBLE, ANYHOW.

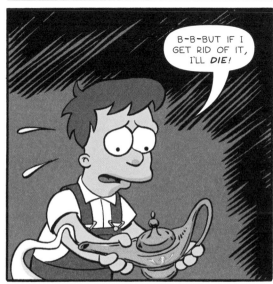

B-B-BUT IF I GET RID OF IT, I'LL *DIE!*

I JUST WISH I'D NEVER FOUND THIS THING!
OHHHHH! I-I DON'T KNOW WHAT TO DO!
D'OH.
POOF!
HEY! MY MISSING DONUT!
CHOMP!
OW!
NO...THIS IS THE DONUT I LOST LAST YEAR!
DEE-LICIOUS!
CHOMP!
OW!
MMMMM...
THE END

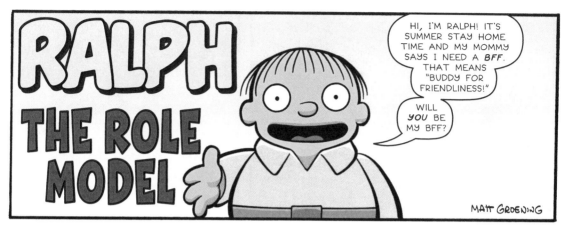

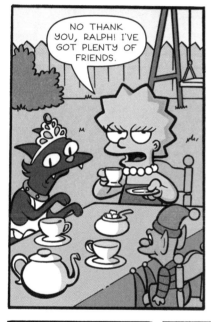

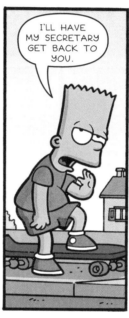

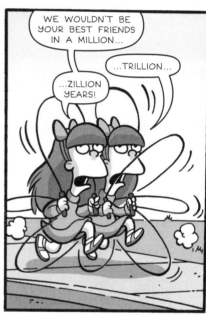

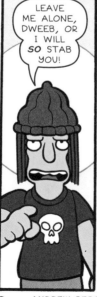

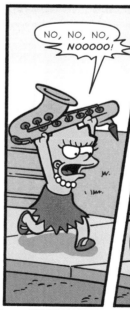

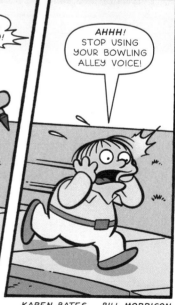

JESSE McCANN
SCRIPT

JAMES LLOYD
PENCILS

ANDREW PEPOY
INKS

ART VILLANUEVA
COLORS

KAREN BATES
LETTERS

BILL MORRISON
EDITOR

I'LL PLAY WITH MY IMAGINE FRIENDS. THEY'RE NEVER BUSY!
MISTER? 'SCUSE ME, MISTER.
WILL YOU HELP ME, MISTER? WILL YOU BE MY ROLE MODEL?
YOU'RE FUNNY. YOU RAIN WHEN YOU TALK!
THAT'S 'CAUSE I'M MISSING TWO TEEF...SEE, MISTER?
I'M RALPH!
WILL YOU BE MY ROLE MODEL, RALPH? PLEEEEASE?
"RALPH" MEANS THROW UP.
I HAVE TO GO INSIDE MY HOUSE NOW.
MOMMY!

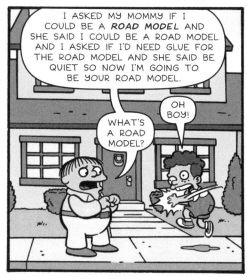

I ASKED MY MOMMY IF I COULD BE A *ROAD MODEL* AND SHE SAID I COULD BE A ROAD MODEL AND I ASKED IF I'D NEED GLUE FOR THE ROAD MODEL AND SHE SAID BE QUIET SO NOW I'M GOING TO BE YOUR ROAD MODEL.

OH BOY!

WHAT'S A ROAD MODEL?

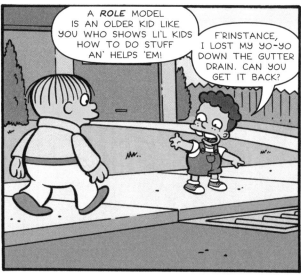

A *ROLE* MODEL IS AN OLDER KID LIKE YOU WHO SHOWS LI'L KIDS HOW TO DO STUFF AN' HELPS 'EM!

F'RINSTANCE, I LOST MY YO-YO DOWN THE GUTTER DRAIN. CAN YOU GET IT BACK?

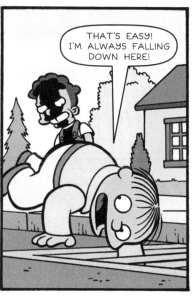

THAT'S EASY! I'M ALWAYS FALLING DOWN HERE!

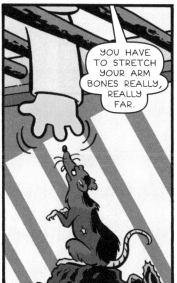

YOU HAVE TO STRETCH YOUR ARM BONES REALLY, REALLY FAR.

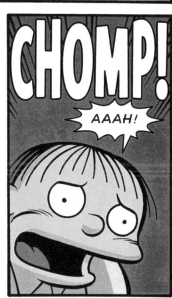

CHOMP!

AAAH!

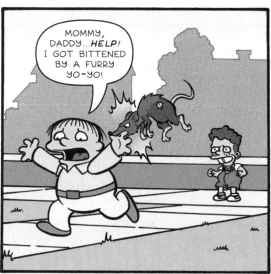

MOMMY, DADDY...*HELP!* I GOT BITTENED BY A FURRY YO-YO!

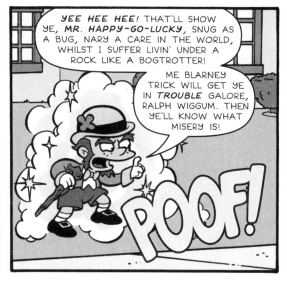

YEE HEE HEE! THAT'LL SHOW YE, *MR. HAPPY-GO-LUCKY,* SNUG AS A BUG, NARY A CARE IN THE WORLD, WHILST I SUFFER LIVIN' UNDER A ROCK LIKE A BOGTROTTER!

ME BLARNEY TRICK WILL GET YE IN *TROUBLE* GALORE, RALPH WIGGUM. THEN YE'LL KNOW WHAT MISERY IS!

POOF!

GOOD BOY, RALPHIE! WE'VE BEEN SCOURING THE SEWERS FOR THIS PLAGUE RAT!
AREN'T YOU GLAD YOU GOT ALL THOSE RABIES SHOTS IN YOUR BELLY?
I'M A HERO!
WHAT?!
FAITH AND BEGORRAH! DAGNABBIT AND DOGGONE IT!
WEE WIGGUM HAS THE LUCK O' THE IRISH! SURE AN' I MUST TRY AGAIN.
WHAT ELSE CAN I TAUGHT YOU?
POOF!
OH! UMM...
...CAN YOU SHOW ME HOW TO PITCH MY BASEBALL?
WHERE DID THOSE COME FROM? YOU MUST HAVE LONG POCKETS!
I'LL STAND OVER HERE, AND YOU TOSS ME SOME ZINGERS!
AH! WHAT'RE YOU DOING? YOU'RE TOO CLOSE!
I'M NOT A GOOD THROWER. GYM TEACHER SAYS I HAVE ARMS LIKE NOODLES!

I'M SURE YOU CAN THROW MY BASEBALL OKAY.
ME MAGICAL BASEBALL, THAT IS! HEE HEE!
PUT ME IN, COACH!
I'M GONNA THROW US A HOME RUN!
SMASH!
TEE-HEE! THAT'LL PUT RALPH'S FAT IN THE FRYER, SURE!
UH-OH! I GAVE THAT HOUSE AN OWIE.
WIG-GUM! DID YOU JUST THROW A BASEBALL THROUGH MY BEDROOM WINDOW?
YES, SUPER INDENTIST CHALMERS. I CAN'T NOT TELL NO LIE.
YOU SAVED MY BACON, RALPH! I OVERSLEPT AND ALMOST MISSED A LIFE-OR-DEATH SCHOOL BOARD MEETING!
MY PET FISH DIED, AND I PUT HIM DOWN THE GARBAGE DISPOSAL.
GRRR! DOGGONE IT!
I'M WONDER WOMAN!
COME OVER HERE.
CHOO-CHOO! NOW I'M THE PAPOOSE!

SHOW ME HOW TO RIDE THIS BICYCLE.
YESSIR, "ENGINEER BILL!"
FIRST YOU CLIMB INTO THE SADDLE AND GRAB THE STEERERS LIKE THIS.
THEN I'LL GIVE YOU A LITTLE PUSH!
LIKE *THIS*?!
SHOVE!
WHISSSH!
OOH! MY TUMMY'S DOING A TOPSY-TURNOVER!
CLACK!
CLANG!
WHEE!
I CAN SEE MY FEET FROM HERE!
WHUMP!
ZOOM!
CRASH!
WHUMP!
SMASH!
POOF!
HEE HEE! THERE'S A GRAND BIT O' TROUBLE FOR YE, SURE!
LET'S SEE YE GET OUTTA *THAT* ONE!

YAY! ***THE LONG RANGER*** CAUGHT ME!
WHAT?!
CAUTION
MOMENTS LATER...
THAT LITTLE BUTTERBALL DUDE LANDED RIGHT ON TOP OF ME!
THAT'S SOME FINE POLICE WORK, SON! MIGHTY FINE.
KID'S A NATURAL, CHIEF.
DOGGONE IT!
DOG BISCUITS TASTE LIKE LIVER AND SAND.
OH, GO AWAY! DAGNABBIT AND DOGGONE!!
I'M SORRY YOUR DOGGIE IS GONE!
DAFT, LUCKY RALPH.
MAY YE BE AFFLICTED WITH AN ITCH, AN' NO NAILS TO SCRATCH IT!
POOF!
HERE, YOU CAN SNUGGLE WITH ***DADDY'S*** POLICE DOGGIES!
F-F-FAITH AN' ME DEAR, SAINTED MUM!
GRRRR!
JAPERS! KEEP AWAY, YE NASTY CURS!
AIEEEE!
HELPING THE LITTLE GUYS, IT'S WHAT I DO!
I'M RALPH...***ROAD MODEL!***
SNARL!
GROWL!
THE END

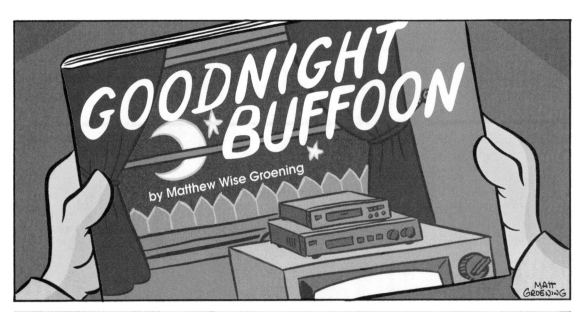

GOODNIGHT BUFFOON

by Matthew Wise Groening

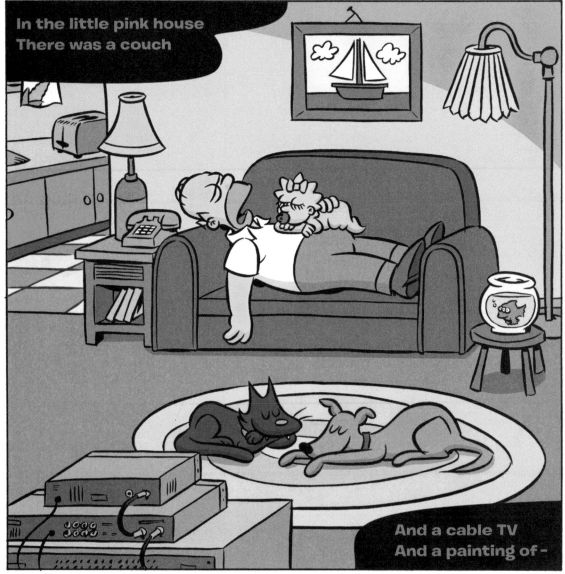

In the little pink house
There was a couch

And a cable TV
And a painting of –

PATRIC M. VERRONE & MAX DAVISON
SCRIPT

MIKE KAZALEH
ART

NATHAN HAMILL
COLORS

KAREN BATES
LETTERS

NATHAN KANE
EDITOR

A sailboat at sea

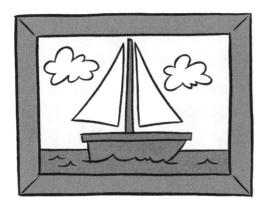

**And three happy elves
Sitting on shelves**

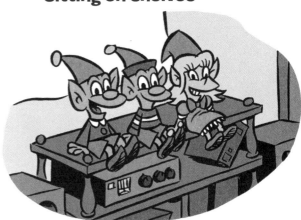

And a four-legged stool

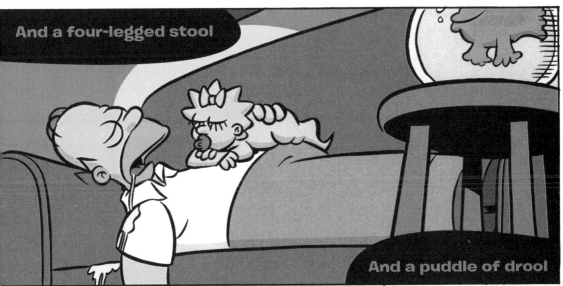

And a puddle of drool

And a cat
And a puppy

And a three-eyed
guppy

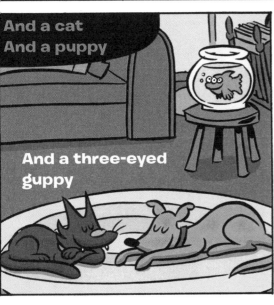

**And a rug and a lamp
And a girl with a bow
On the gut of a fat man
muttering...**

D'OH!

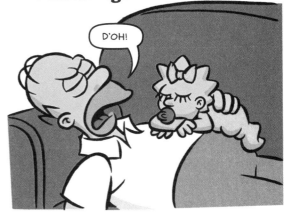

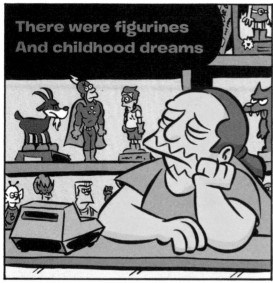

There were figurines
And childhood dreams

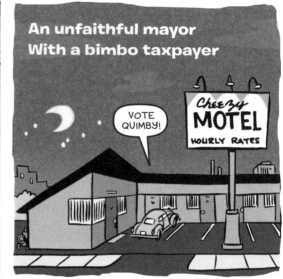

An unfaithful mayor
With a bimbo taxpayer

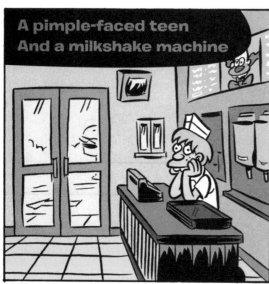

A pimple-faced teen
And a milkshake machine

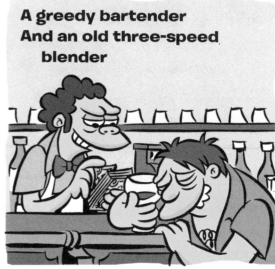

A greedy bartender
And an old three-speed
blender

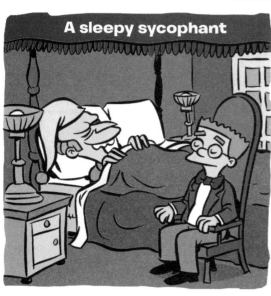

A sleepy sycophant

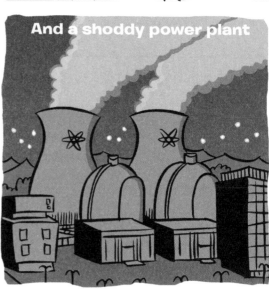

And a shoddy power plant

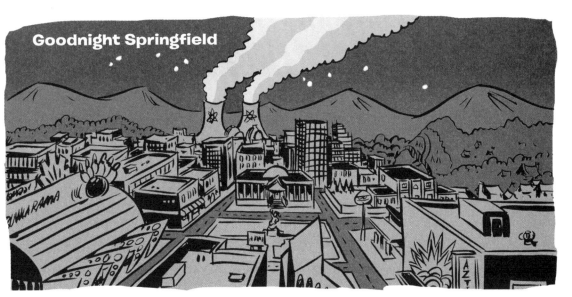

Goodnight Springfield

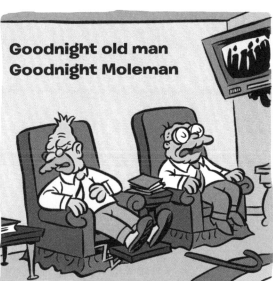

Goodnight old man
Goodnight Moleman

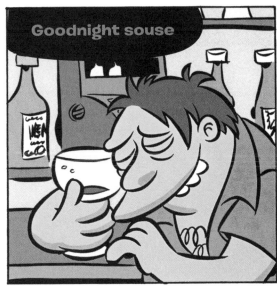

Goodnight souse

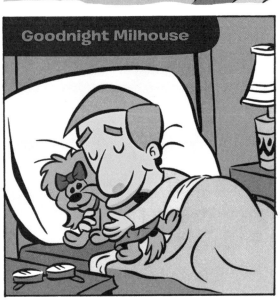

Goodnight Milhouse

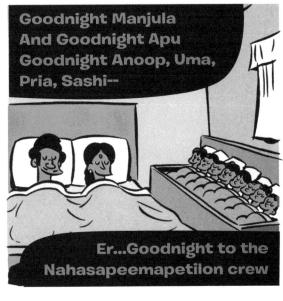

Goodnight Manjula
And Goodnight Apu
Goodnight Anoop, Uma,
Pria, Sashi--

Er...Goodnight to the
Nahasapeemapetilon crew

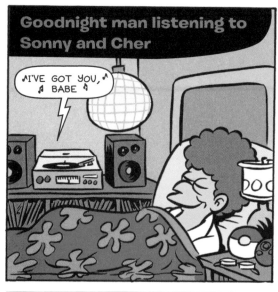

Goodnight man listening to Sonny and Cher

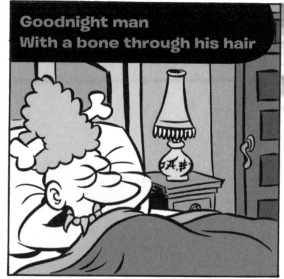

Goodnight man
With a bone through his hair

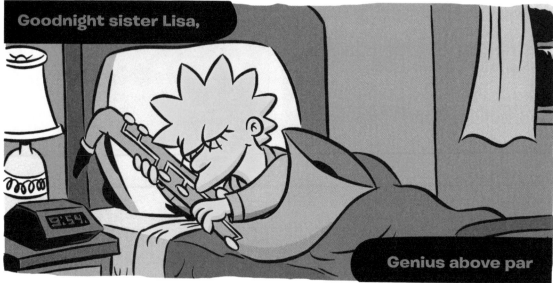

Goodnight sister Lisa,

Genius above par

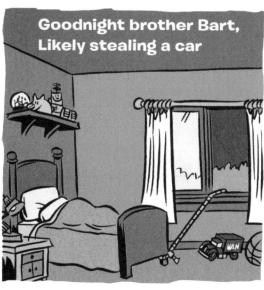

Goodnight brother Bart,
Likely stealing a car

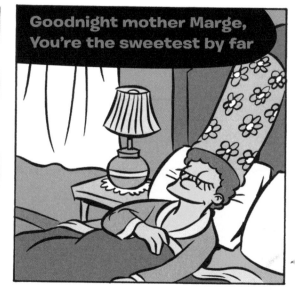

Goodnight mother Marge,
You're the sweetest by far

Goodnight house
Goodnight couch
Goodnight kitty
Goodnight to the whole city
Goodnight fish and lamp and wall
Goodnight babies,
Big and small

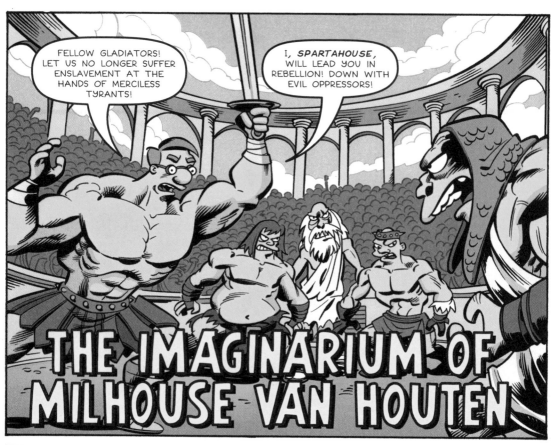

FELLOW GLADIATORS! LET US NO LONGER SUFFER ENSLAVEMENT AT THE HANDS OF MERCILESS TYRANTS!

I, *SPARTAHOUSE*, WILL LEAD YOU IN REBELLION! DOWN WITH EVIL OPPRESSORS!

THE IMAGINARIUM OF MILHOUSE VAN HOUTEN

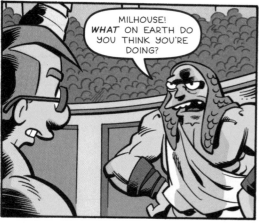

MILHOUSE! *WHAT* ON EARTH DO YOU THINK YOU'RE DOING?

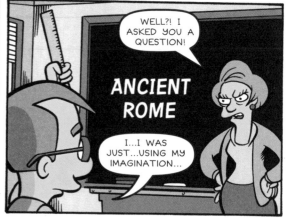

WELL?! I ASKED YOU A QUESTION!

ANCIENT ROME

I...I WAS JUST...USING MY IMAGINATION...

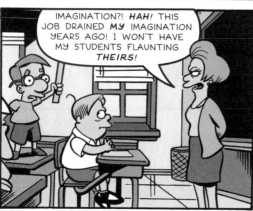

IMAGINATION?! *HAH!* THIS JOB DRAINED *MY* IMAGINATION YEARS AGO! I WON'T HAVE MY STUDENTS FLAUNTING *THEIRS!*

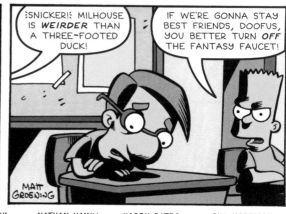

⌇SNICKER!⌇ MILHOUSE IS *WEIRDER* THAN A THREE-FOOTED DUCK!

IF WE'RE GONNA STAY BEST FRIENDS, DOOFUS, YOU BETTER TURN *OFF* THE FANTASY FAUCET!

PAT MCGREAL
SCRIPT

JOHN DELANEY
PENCILS

ANDREW PEPOY
INKS

NATHAN HAMILL
COLORS

KAREN BATES
LETTERS

BILL MORRISON
EDITOR

SOON...
I'VE GOT A REPUTATION TO MAINTAIN! HANGING OUT WITH YOU COULD *RUIN* ME!
IT'S TRUE! I'M A LAUGHING STOCK BECAUSE I CAN'T CONTROL MY IMAGINATION!
BUT AT LEAST *YOU'RE* STILL MY FRIEND, BART! WE'RE A *TEAM!* LIKE INSEPARABLE ADVENTURERS EXPLORING AN UNTAMED WILDERNESS...
MILHOUSE! DON'T DO IT!
I SAY, OLD MAN! PERHAPS WE'LL BAG A BIT OF BIG GAME TODAY, EH WOT?
GIVE ME A BREAK! I DON'T WANT TO BE PART OF THIS DAYDREAM!
LOOK! A GREAT *GRIZZLY!* HE'S PROBABLY *RAVENOUS* AFTER MONTHS OF HIBERNATION!
DON'T WORRY, BART! I'LL PROTECT YOU FROM THAT BIG SMELLY BRUTE!
HEY! WHO ARE YOU CALLIN' A BIG SMELLY BRUTE?!
BRAAAP!
I...I WAS JUST USING MY IMAGINATION!
GET REAL, POINDEXTER! IMAGINATION IS FOR *LOSERS!*
HAW HAW! CHECK OUT THOSE DWEEBS! PLAYING "*PRETEND*" LIKE A COUPLE OF BABIES!
THAT'S THE LAST STRAW! THIS FRIENDSHIP IS *OVER!*

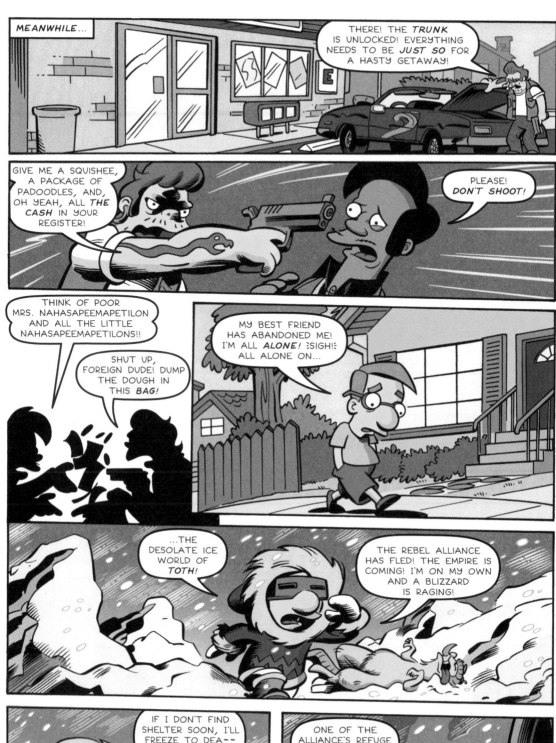

MEANWHILE...

THERE! THE *TRUNK* IS UNLOCKED! EVERYTHING NEEDS TO BE *JUST SO* FOR A HASTY GETAWAY!

GIVE ME A SQUISHEE, A PACKAGE OF PADOODLES, AND, OH YEAH, ALL *THE CASH* IN YOUR REGISTER!

PLEASE! *DON'T SHOOT!*

THINK OF POOR MRS. NAHASAPEEMAPETILON AND ALL THE LITTLE NAHASAPEEMAPETILONS!!

SHUT UP, FOREIGN DUDE! DUMP THE DOUGH IN THIS *BAG!*

MY BEST FRIEND HAS ABANDONED ME! I'M ALL *ALONE!* ≶SIGH!≶ ALL ALONE ON...

...THE DESOLATE ICE WORLD OF *TOTH!*

THE REBEL ALLIANCE HAS FLED! THE EMPIRE IS COMING! I'M ON MY OWN AND A BLIZZARD IS RAGING!

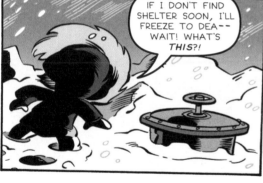

IF I DON'T FIND SHELTER SOON, I'LL FREEZE TO DEA-- WAIT! WHAT'S *THIS*?!

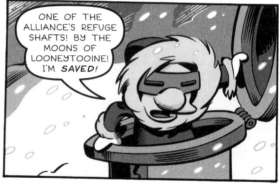

ONE OF THE ALLIANCE'S REFUGE SHAFTS! BY THE MOONS OF LOONEYTOOINE! I'M *SAVED!*

PIECE O' CAKE! THIS HAUL'LL PAY FOR AN ***ARMFUL*** OF TATTOOS EASY!
?
SLAM!
TIME TO PUT THE PEDAL TO THE METAL!
HEY!
VRRROOOOM!
OPEN UP! LET ME OUT OF HERE!
WHAM!
BANG!
WHAT'S THAT ANNOYING ***NOISE?*** IS MY MUFFLER SHOT?! BETTER CHECK IT OUT!
HOLY COW! THIS THING IS FILLED WITH MONEY! A ***FORTUNE!*** IT...IT'S LIKE...
GAS
...I'M A DEEP SEA DIVER WHO'S DISCOVERED A PIRATE'S ***TREASURE*** IN THE HULL OF A SUNKEN GALLEON!
UGH! A ***BEAST*** FROM THE DEEP! GUARDING ITS GOLD! ENSNARING ME IN SLITHERY TENTACLES!

LET GO OF THAT STASH, YOU LITTLE DOOFUS!
NEVER!
I FOUND IT FAIR AND SQUARE! IT'S MINE!
GAH! YOU'RE MAKING ME MAD!
AW, LOOK. SOME BIG GUY IS TRYING TO STUFF A LITTLE KID INTO THE TRUNK OF HIS CAR! AIN'T THAT CUTE!
RRIIP!
OH WOW. BUMMER.
HMM. WHAT'S A PUNK LIKE HIM DOING WITH THAT KIND OF DOUGH?
PUBLISHERS CLEARING HOUSE SWEEPSTAKES?
WAIT! REMEMBER THAT APB WE GOT? THE KWIK-E-MART WAS KNOCKED OVER!
RIGHT! IT MUST BE STOLEN LOOT! WE GOTTA APPREHEND THAT PERP!
SOON AS WE FINISH OUR DONUTS AND COFFEE.
RIGHT. ANOTHER REFILL, CHIEF?

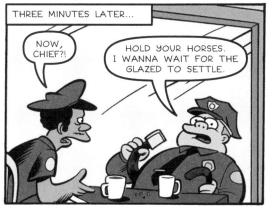

THREE MINUTES LATER...

NOW, CHIEF?!

HOLD YOUR HORSES. I WANNA WAIT FOR THE GLAZED TO SETTLE.

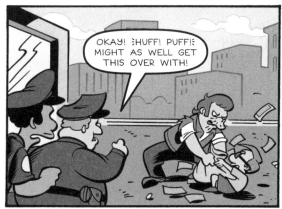

OKAY! ¡HUFF! PUFF!¡ MIGHT AS WELL GET THIS OVER WITH!

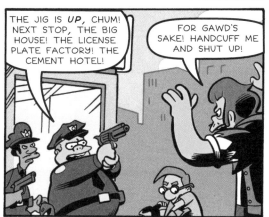

THE JIG IS *UP,* CHUM! NEXT STOP, THE BIG HOUSE! THE LICENSE PLATE FACTORY! THE CEMENT HOTEL!

FOR GAWD'S SAKE! HANDCUFF ME AND SHUT UP!

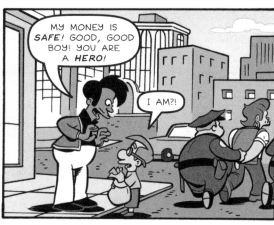

MY MONEY IS *SAFE!* GOOD, GOOD BOY! YOU ARE A *HERO!*

I AM?!

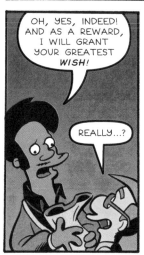

OH, YES, INDEED! AND AS A REWARD, I WILL GRANT YOUR GREATEST *WISH!*

REALLY...?

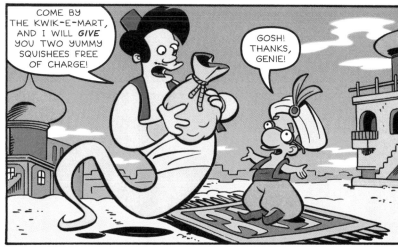

COME BY THE KWIK-E-MART, AND I WILL *GIVE* YOU TWO YUMMY SQUISHEES FREE OF CHARGE!

GOSH! THANKS, GENIE!

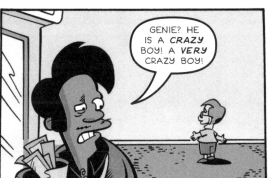

GENIE? HE IS A *CRAZY* BOY! A *VERY* CRAZY BOY!

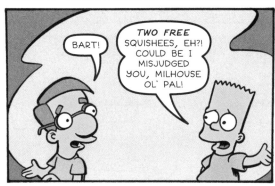

BART!

TWO FREE SQUISHEES, EH?! COULD BE I MISJUDGED YOU, MILHOUSE OL' PAL!

MMMMMMM! SWEET OVERSTIMULATING SUGARY GOODNESS!
DOES THIS MEAN WE'RE BEST FRIENDS AGAIN, BART?
MAYBE. PROVIDED YOU SLIP THIS INTO MRS. KRABAPPEL'S DESK!
KROAK!
ALL RIGHT, YOU INSUFFERABLE MICROBES! I KNOW SPARTAHOUSE IS RESPONSIBLE FOR THIS APPALLINGLY JUVENILE PRANK!
THE QUESTION IS...WHICH ONE OF YOU IS SPARTAHOUSE?!
I AM SPARTAHOUSE!
NO WAY! I AM SPARTAHOUSE!
FORGET IT! I AM SPARTAHOUSE!
AT LAST! I AM ACCEPTED AND PROTECTED BY MY PEERS!
OH, WHAT THE HECK! IT'S HIM!
SIGH!
THE END

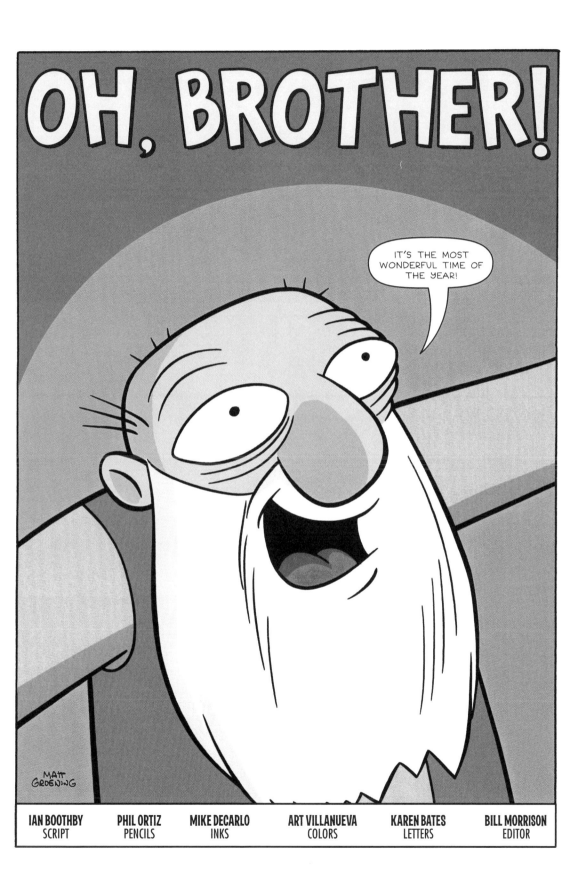

OH, BROTHER!

IT'S THE MOST WONDERFUL TIME OF THE YEAR!

MATT GROENING

| **IAN BOOTHBY** SCRIPT | **PHIL ORTIZ** PENCILS | **MIKE DECARLO** INKS | **ART VILLANUEVA** COLORS | **KAREN BATES** LETTERS | **BILL MORRISON** EDITOR |

ELECTION TIME!
HELLO, OLD PEOPLE. AS YOU...ER, AH...KNOW, YOU ARE THE ONLY DEMOGRAPHIC THAT VOTES WITH ANY REGULARITY.
SO, I AM HERE TO PANDER! WHAT CAN I DO FOR YOU ALL TODAY?
OBITUARIES
SOON...
THAT'S THE STUFF! WORK THE ARCH, QUIMBY!
YES, SIR!
NOW, JUST WAIT A GUL' DANGED MINUTE!
WAIT YOUR TURN, ABE!
EVERY ELECTION WE GET QUIMBY TO LISTEN TO OUR STORIES, RUB OUR FEET, AND CLEAN OUR GUTTERS!
BUT WE NEVER GET WHAT WE REALLY WANT.
AND THAT IS?
FORCE OUR FAMILIES TO SPEND TIME WITH US!

AND SO I AM...ER... DECLARING TOMORROW "TAKE YOUR PARENT TO WORK DAY!"
DVD
THIS IS A MANDATORY HOLIDAY. FAILURE TO COMPLY WILL RESULT IN A FLOGGING!
AW, I HATE ELECTION SEASON!
AND SO...
DAD, THIS IS MY STORE, THE LEFTORIUM.
DIG IT, MAN! MY SQUARE OF A SON IS FINALLY GETTING INTO THE GROOVE!
MY LITTLE BIRD IS FINALLY FLYING ON THE LEFT SIDE OF POLITICS!
SALE
THAT'S NOT WHAT THIS STORE IS ABOUT. IT'S...
HEY, BIG DADDY! ALL THIS STUFF IS LIKE, **FREE** MAN! TAKE WHAT YOU WANT! EACH TO HIS OWN NEEDS!
I AM NOT LEFT-HANDED, BUT AT THESE PRICES, I CAN **LEARN** TO BE!
NO, WAIT!
HEY, EVERYONE! EVERYTHING'S ***FREE***!
SALE
SO, LIKE, WHEN'S OUR COFFEE BREAK, MAN?
HONOR THY MOTHER AND FATHER. HONOR THY MOTHER AND FATHER.
WE HONOR MOST CREDIT

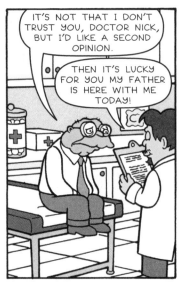

IT'S NOT THAT I DON'T TRUST YOU, DOCTOR NICK, BUT I'D LIKE A SECOND OPINION.

THEN IT'S LUCKY FOR YOU MY FATHER IS HERE WITH ME TODAY!

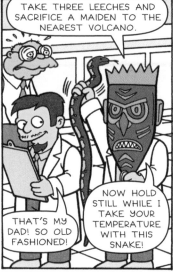

TAKE THREE LEECHES AND SACRIFICE A MAIDEN TO THE NEAREST VOLCANO.

THAT'S MY DAD! SO OLD FASHIONED!

NOW HOLD STILL WHILE I TAKE YOUR TEMPERATURE WITH THIS SNAKE!

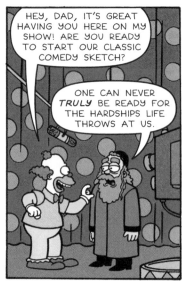

HEY, DAD, IT'S GREAT HAVING YOU HERE ON MY SHOW! ARE YOU READY TO START OUR CLASSIC COMEDY SKETCH?

ONE CAN NEVER *TRULY* BE READY FOR THE HARDSHIPS LIFE THROWS AT US.

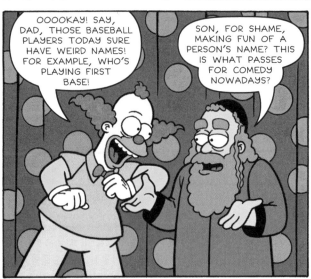

OOOOKAY! SAY, DAD, THOSE BASEBALL PLAYERS TODAY SURE HAVE WEIRD NAMES! FOR EXAMPLE, WHO'S PLAYING FIRST BASE!

SON, FOR SHAME, MAKING FUN OF A PERSON'S NAME? THIS IS WHAT PASSES FOR COMEDY NOWADAYS?

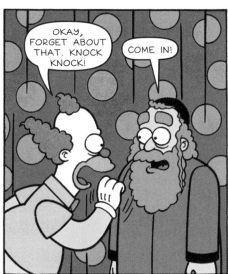

OKAY, FORGET ABOUT THAT. KNOCK KNOCK!

COME IN!

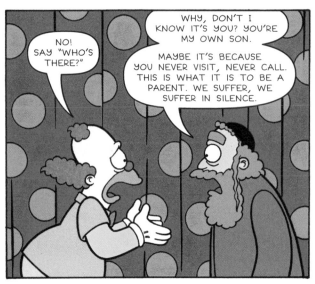

NO! SAY "WHO'S THERE?"

WHY, DON'T I KNOW IT'S YOU? YOU'RE MY OWN SON.

MAYBE IT'S BECAUSE YOU NEVER VISIT, NEVER CALL. THIS IS WHAT IT IS TO BE A PARENT. WE SUFFER, WE SUFFER IN SILENCE.

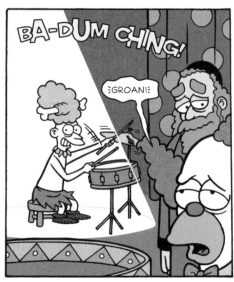

BA-DUM CHING!

≒GROAN!≒

ROOM 122
OKAY, DAD, YOU HAVE TO PROMISE NOT TO TOUCH ANY-THING. THIS IS A HIGHLY TECHNICAL PLACE WITH THINGS YOU WOULDN'T UNDERSTAND!
OH, AND *YOU* DO?
SECTOR 7G
THIS ISN'T ABOUT ME! ONCE YOU LEARN HOW TO PROGRAM YOUR VCR, WE'LL TALK!
WHAT'LL WE DO FIRST? GO ON A TOUR OF THE PLACE?
YOU'RE GOING TO STAND THERE, AND I'M GOING TO READ THIS SAFETY MANUAL!
BUT I THOUGHT WE COULD...
SAFETY MANUAL
SIGH!
ZZZZZZ!
SAFETY MANUAL
MAYBE THIS THING PICKS UP THAT OLD-TIMEY RADIO STATION I LIKE!
CLICK!
CLACK!
CLICK!
UH-OH!
WARNING! MELTDOWN! MELTDOWN! EVACUATE IMMEDIATELY!
ZZZZZZ!
SAFETY MANUAL
ABANDON ALL HOPE! MELTDOWN!

BETTER JUST KEEP PUSHING BUTTONS!
I COULDN'T MAKE THINGS *WORSE!*
CLICK!
CLICK!
CLICK!
WARNING! THINGS ARE NOW MUCH WORSE!
YAAAH!
CLACK!
CLACK!
CLACK!
MELTDOWN AVERTED! RETURN TO WORK!
WHEW!
YAWN! DID YOU HEAR SOMETHING?
NOPE!
YOU KNOW, I USED TO FIND MELT-DOWNS STRESSFUL, BUT NOW I THINK THEY'RE A NICE BREAK IN THE DAY.
YEAH, IT GIVES ME AN EXCUSE TO... WHATAYACALLIT?... PRACTICE MY DEATH BED REPENTANCE!
MEANWHILE, AT SPRINGFIELD ELEMENTARY...
SPRINGFIELD ELEMENTARY SCHOOL
MICE! MICE! THEY'RE EVERYWHERE, *EVERYWHERE!*
ACH! WEE BART SIMPSON STRIKES AGAIN!

WELL PLAYED, OLD MAN!
HA!
THE REAL TRICK WAS FILLING THE SUBSTITUTE TEACHER'S POCKETS WITH CHEESE WHILE HE WASN'T LOOKING!
HA!
HA!
HA!
HA!
WELL, I HOPE YOU'RE HAPPY. THAT WAS THE LAST SUBSTITUTE TEACHER AVAILABLE. THANKS TO WHOEVER DID THAT PRANK, YOU ALL AREN'T GOING TO LEARN ANYTHING FOR THE REST OF THE DAY!
YAY!
WOOO!
YAHOOO!
THAT WASN'T THE REACTION I WAS HOPING FOR.
STAND ASIDE, MILKSOP!
MOTHER! YOU CAN'T BOSS ME AROUND AT SCHOOL, ONLY AT HOME!
SCREEEE!
YOU NEED A SUBSTITUTE TEACHER? I'LL TEACH YOUR CLASS!
YAAAAAAH!
BART, MAYBE YOU SHOULD LEAVE THIS ONE ALONE.
AU CONTRAIRE, MILHOUSE. I'LL BREAK HER SPIRIT BY SECOND RECESS!

THIS DANG AUTOMAT DON'T WORK! I PUT MY QUARTERS IN FOR A HAM SANDWICH AND NOTHING HAPPENED!
MR. SIMPSON, THAT'S A MICROWAVE!
WAIT, *NOW* IT'S DOING SOMETHING!
BING!
WHIRRRRRR!
WAIT, DID YOU SAY YOU PUT METAL IN THERE?
LUNCH ROOM
EMPLOYEE LUNCH ROOM
BLAAAAM!
WOW! THAT'S BETTER THAN TWO CUPS OF COFFEE FOR STARTING UP THE OLD TICKER!
YOU'RE AN EMBARRASSMENT TO THE FAMILY NAME, MONTY!
BUT, MOTHER, I'M A ***BILLIONAIRE!***
OTHER BOYS YOUR AGE ARE ***TRILLIONAIRES!***
WHAT ARE YOU STARING AT, POPS?
LAYOFFS
NOW, NOW, MONTY. LEAVE THE HANDSOME YOUNG MAN ALONE!
HANDSOME?
YOUNG?
MAN?

BACK AT SPRINGFIELD ELEMENTARY...
WELL, NOW THAT WE'RE BACK FROM RECESS WE'LL START OFF WITH SOME HISTORY. LET ME JUST SEE IF THE LAST TEACHER LEFT BEHIND ANY NOTES.
YAAAAH!
RIBBIT!
HA! HA! HA! HA!
YES! THAT COULDN'T HAVE GONE BETTER!
HA!
HA!
HA!
I NEED TO WRITE THIS DOWN IN MY PRANK JOURNAL!
YAAAAAAH!
RIBBIT!
RIBBIT!
RIBBIT!
RIBBIT!
THAT'S RIGHT! I HANDLE PRANKS THE CHICAGO WAY! PUT A FROG IN MY DESK AT RECESS I PUT A DOZEN IN YOURS.
HA! HA!
RIBBIT!
HA!
HA!
THIS... ISN'T...OVER.

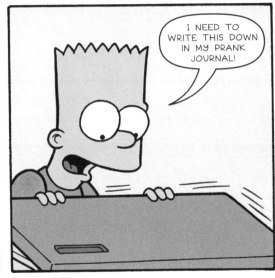

I GOT YOU A TEA. IT'S THE ONLY THING IN THIS PLACE I KNOW HOW TO MAKE.
HOW SWEET! THANK YOU.
I HAVE TO APOLOGIZE FOR HOW MY SON YELLED AT YOU. HE'S JUST UPSET AT BEING A DISAPPOINTMENT TO ME.
YOUR SON'S A DISAPPOINTMENT? MINE, TOO! WE HAVE SO MUCH IN COMMON. WOULD YOU LIKE TO HAVE DINNER AND TALK ABOUT WHERE THEY BOTH WENT WRONG?
I'D BE DELIGHTED!
MR. BURNS, YOUR MOTHER HAS LEFT THE BUILDING.
GOOD! I CAN FINALLY STOP HOLDING IN MY STOMACH!
THAT'S BETTER!
SHE LEFT WITH ABRAHAM SIMPSON, SIR.
SEND HIM A CONDOLENCE BOUQUET!
MEANWHILE...
BRRRRRING!

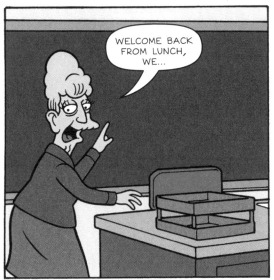

WELCOME BACK FROM LUNCH, WE...

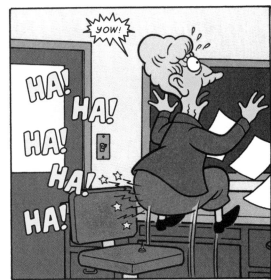

YOW!

HA! HA! HA! HA! HA!

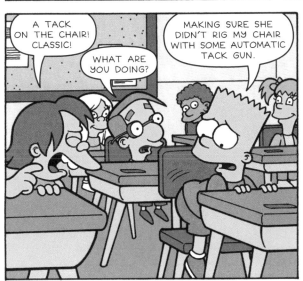

A TACK ON THE CHAIR! CLASSIC!

WHAT ARE YOU DOING?

MAKING SURE SHE DIDN'T RIG MY CHAIR WITH SOME AUTOMATIC TACK GUN.

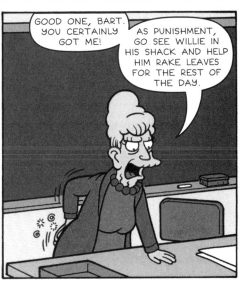

GOOD ONE, BART. YOU CERTAINLY GOT ME!

AS PUNISHMENT, GO SEE WILLIE IN HIS SHACK AND HELP HIM RAKE LEAVES FOR THE REST OF THE DAY.

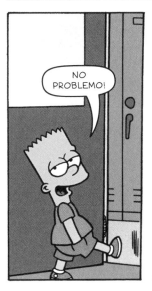

NO PROBLEMO!

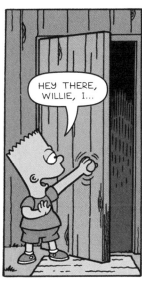

HEY THERE, WILLIE, I...

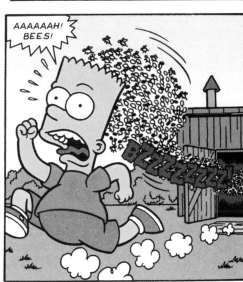

AAAAAAH! BEES!

BZZZZZZZ

STING ME ONCE, SHAME ON YOU. STING YOU A HUNDRED TIMES, GOOD ON ME!
GRUNT!
THAT WAS A NICE BIT O' PRANK REVENGE!
THANKS!
BUT NEXT TIME CANNA YE GIVE WILLIE SOME WARNIN'?
WALK IT OFF, SCOTTY!
THE NEXT DAY...
BART, CAN YOU TAKE YOUR REVENGE PLANS OFF THE TABLE FOR BREAKFAST?
WE REALLY NEED TO GET A TABLE JUST FOR REVENGE SCHEMES.

GRAMPA? WHY ARE YOU SO DRESSED UP?
GREAT NEWS!
I HIT IT OFF WITH THAT SWEET THING, MRS. BURNS!
SWEET LIKE AN OLD PRUNE, YOU MEAN?
SHE'S A BIT OF AN OLD-FASHIONED GAL AND WOULDN'T LET ME KISS HER UNTIL WE WERE MARRIED.
SO...
GASP!
WE GOT HITCHED! MEET YOUR NEW MOTHER AND GRANDMOTHER!
ABRAHAM, WE NEED TO LEAVE NOW FOR OUR HONEYMOON.
HONEYMOON? WHERE?
JUST A WALK AROUND THE MALL AND THE EARLY BIRD SPECIAL AT THE PANCAKE HOUSE! SEE YA!

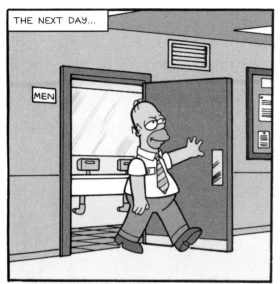

THE NEXT DAY...

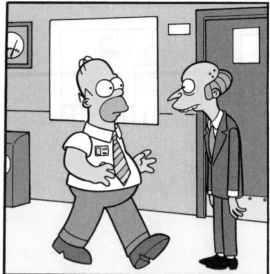

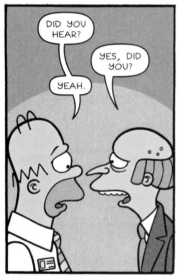

DID YOU HEAR?

YES, DID YOU?

YEAH.

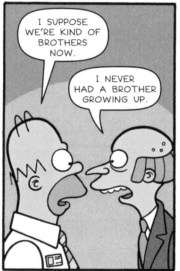

I SUPPOSE WE'RE KIND OF BROTHERS NOW.

I NEVER HAD A BROTHER GROWING UP.

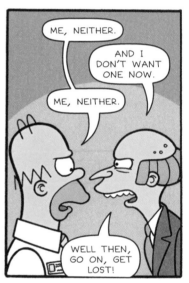

ME, NEITHER.

AND I DON'T WANT ONE NOW.

ME, NEITHER.

WELL THEN, GO ON, GET LOST!

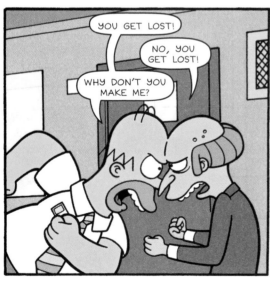

YOU GET LOST!

NO, YOU GET LOST!

WHY DON'T YOU MAKE ME?

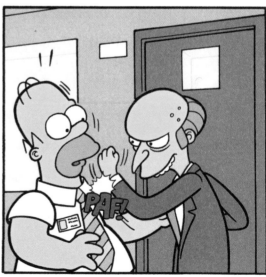

P4F!

MR. BURNS! DEAR HEAVEN!
SIMPSON! STOP THAT AT ONCE!
OH, NOT TO WORRY, SMITHERS.
I WAS JUST ENGAGING IN SOME GOOD-NATURED ROUGH-HOUSING WITH MY BROTHER.
THAT WAS KINDA FUN! WANNA HANG OUT SOMETIME?
INDEED. BUT FIRST, SMITHERS, BE A LAMB AND CALL AN AMBULANCE. MOST OF MY INTERNAL ORGANS HAVE BURST!
I'M SO SORRY!
TUT TUT! THIS IS WHAT I BOUGHT ALL THOSE STEM CELLS FOR. I'LL BE RIGHT AS RAIN BY MORNING!
MRS. SKINNER, THIS IS HARD FOR ME TO SAY...
...BUT YOU WIN. CAN WE CALL A TRUCE?
OF COURSE. THERE'S NO SHAME IN LOSING TO A SMARTER FOE!
CAN I HAVE A HUG?

OF COURSE, SWEETIE!
HA HA! SUCKER!
Kick ME
I'M GETTING A TEXT MESSAGE.
ME, TOO!
BEEP!
BOOP!
BLEEP!
IT'S FROM BART. IT SAYS "KICK ME!"
WAIT! I DIDN'T SAY THAT!
WHO AM I SUPPOSED TO BELIEVE, YOU OR THE TEXT? PRINT DOESN'T LIE!
OH DEAR, COULD SOMEONE HAVE TYPED THAT INTO THE PHONE IN YOUR POCKET DURING A FAKE HUG? NO, THAT COULDN'T BE IT.
SPRINGFIELD ELEMENTARY SCHOOL
GET HIM!
I CALL HIS TORSO!
SAVE HIS SHINS FOR ME!
YAAAAAAAAH!

THE NEXT DAY...
HEY THERE, BROTHER! FORGET ABOUT WORK AND COME WITH ME!
WHAT ARE WE DOING?
EVERYTHING I NEVER GOT TO DO AS AN ONLY CHILD!
I HAVE SOME CLOTHES FOR YOU IN MY OFFICE!
KICK THE CAN!
WHAT'S SO FUN ABOUT THAT?
THWACK!
HA! THAT *IS* FUN!
OW-DIDDLY-*OW*!
ROLLING A **BARREL HOOP**!
AW NO, **MY PICKLES**! I'D BEEN SAVING THOSE FOR YEARS. THEY WERE MY **NEST EGG**!
OL' GIL'S GONNA NEED A BAILOUT!

WHAT NOW?
WE PICK A FIGHT WITH SOME OTHER BROTHERS!
SPRINGFIELD MUSIC HALL TONIGHT THE SMOTHERS BROTHERS
CELEBRITY ENTRANCE
MAN, A BOARD WITH A NAIL IN IT IS NO MATCH FOR AN UPRIGHT BASS.
SO NOTED.
AND NOW, A CLASSIC BROTHERLY JAPE! KNOCKING ON DOORS AND RUNNING AWAY!
KNOCK! KNOCK!
NOW, RUN AS FAST AS YOUR LEGS WILL CARRY YOU!
TEE HEE!
OH, MY KNEES! I SHOULD HAVE REFILLED THEM WITH FLUID!
GASP! WHEEZE!
ARE YOU TWO ALL RIGHT? WOULD YOU LIKE TO COME IN FOR A LEMONADE?
GASP! YES!

HELLO, BART.
MRS. SKINNER! THIS ISN'T WHAT IT LOOKS LIKE!
YOU WEREN'T GOING TO DRESS UP AS ME AND PUT EMBARRASSING VIDEOS ON THE INTERNET?
NO.
I THOUGHT YOU SAID WE *WERE*.
WILL YOU GET OUTTA HERE?!
HEY, KID, I LIKE YOU. YOU REMIND ME OF ME WHEN I WAS YOUR AGE.
SO I'M GOING TO GROW UP TO BE AN OLD WOMAN? GREAT.
I WAS THE PRANK QUEEN OF MY SCHOOL. I'VE HAD DECADES OF EXPERIENCE SINCE THEN. YOU CAN'T BEAT ME.
WELL, I'M THE PRANK KING OF *THIS* SCHOOL. AT LEAST I *WAS*. WITHOUT *THAT*...
...I'M JUST ANOTHER DUMB KID.
LISTEN UP, KID, I'VE GOT AN IDEA.

HELLO, SEYMOUR. WHAT'S WITH THE GET UP? GOING TO A FUNERAL FOR YOUR HOPES AND DREAMS?
OH HELLO, MOTHER. I'LL HAVE YOU KNOW, THE SPRINGFIELD SHOPPER NEWSPAPER IS TAKING A PICTURE OF ME TODAY FOR AN ARTICLE ABOUT THE MOST DIGNIFIED SCHOOL PRINCIPALS.
BRRRRRING!
GASP! THE FIRE ALARM!
I SUPPOSE WE SHOULD WALK IN AN ORDERLY FASHION TO THE NEAREST EXIT.
THAT'S JUST WHAT WE TELL THE STUDENTS SO THEY WON'T GET IN OUR WAY WHEN THERE'S A ***REAL*** EMERGENCY!
RUN FOR YOUR LIFE! IT'S EVERY STAFF MEMBER FOR THEMSELVES!
AAAH! WHY IS THIS FLOOR SO FRESHLY WAXED? IT'S NOT HOT WAX WEDNESDAY!
SWIIIIISH!
THWACK!
OOOF!
THE SCHOOL MASCOT OUTFIT FOR HOT DOG THURSDAYS?
THIS SHOULD BE IN THE CAFETERIA! WHY WAS IT HANGING BY THE FRONT DOOR?

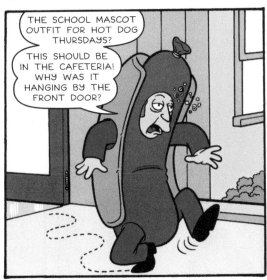

RINGFIELD ELEMENTARY SCHOOL
OH, NO! OH, NO!
SPRINGFIELD ELEMENTARY Home of PRINCIPAL WIENER
WHAT A PICTURE!
PAGE ONE MATERIAL, FOR SURE!
HA! HA! HA!
THE SPRINGFIELD SHOPPER
HA! HA! HA! HA!
THAT WAS AMAZING! WHO THOUGHT OF IT?
BART DID. HE'S THE PRANK KING!
WITH HELP FROM MRS. SKINNER, STILL THE PRANK QUEEN!
GET AWAY! BAD DOG!
HA! HA! HA!
BARK! BARK! BARK!

WHAT A JOLLY TIME WE HAD...EH, BROTHER?
YOU SAID IT, BROTHER!
I'VE TAKEN THE LIBERTY OF ORDERING US A FEW DOZEN MATCHING OUTFITS, TAILOR-MADE, OF COURSE.
WOW, MARGE USUALLY HAS TO BUY MY PANTS FROM CIRCUS SUPPLY STORES!
SAY, THIS IS KIND OF AWKWARD, BUT DURING ONE OF HIS THREATENING PHONE CALLS, I WAS TALKING TO MY BANKER ABOUT US BEING BROTHERS, AND HE WANTED TO KNOW IF...
...BY BEING MY YOUNGEST HEIR, YOU'D INHERIT MY VAST FORTUNE WHEN I PASS ON? OF COURSE.
THAT'S WHAT I TOLD HIM.
HOMER, ARE YOU THINKING OF WAYS TO DO AWAY WITH ME AND MAKE IT LOOK LIKE AN ACCIDENT?
YES, SIR.
HA! I'D BE THINKING EXACTLY THE SAME THING. YOU TRULY *ARE* MY BROTHER!
NO, HE'S NOT!

DAD?
SMITHERS? WHAT'S THE MEANING OF THIS?
I HAVE A CONFESSION TO MAKE, SIR. YOUR MOTHER ISN'T **REALLY** YOUR MOTHER.
EXPLAIN YOUR BABBLING FORTHWITH!
I TRIED TO BRING YOUR **REAL** MOTHER TO THE POWER PLANT FOR "BRING YOUR PARENTS TO WORK DAY."
BUT SHE'S EITHER NOT SPEAKING TO YOU OR DEAD. THE DOCTOR ISN'T ALLOWED TO CHECK BECAUSE OF A CLAUSE IN HER LIVING WILL.
SO I HIRED AN ACTRESS, DAME TALLULAH WINKELMAN, TO INSULT AND BERATE YOU JUST LIKE YOUR REAL MOTHER ALWAYS DID!
CHARMED!
I SHOULD HAVE EXPECTED SOMETHING WAS WRONG WHEN I HAD TO GIVE TEN PERCENT OF OUR WEDDING PRESENTS TO HER AGENT.
AND OUR PRE-NUP ARRANGEMENT ONLY GAVE OUR MARRIAGE A ONE-WEEK RUN.

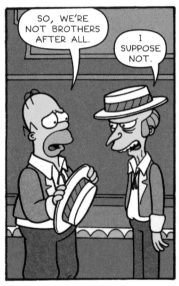

SO, WE'RE NOT BROTHERS AFTER ALL.

I SUPPOSE NOT.

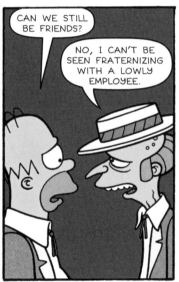

CAN WE STILL BE FRIENDS?

NO, I CAN'T BE SEEN FRATERNIZING WITH A LOWLY EMPLOYEE.

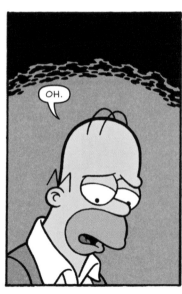

OH.

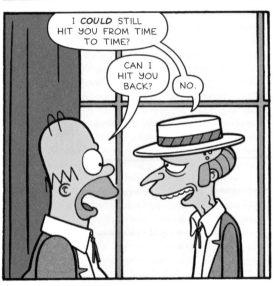

I *COULD* STILL HIT YOU FROM TIME TO TIME?

CAN I HIT YOU BACK?

NO.

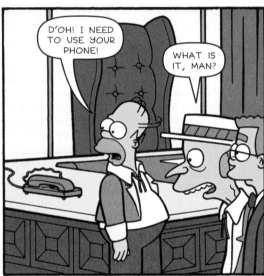

D'OH! I NEED TO USE YOUR PHONE!

WHAT IS IT, MAN?

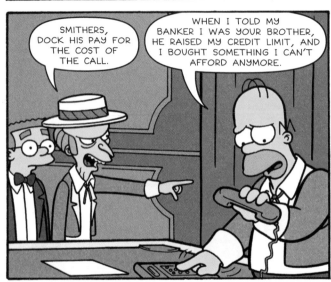

SMITHERS, DOCK HIS PAY FOR THE COST OF THE CALL.

WHEN I TOLD MY BANKER I WAS YOUR BROTHER, HE RAISED MY CREDIT LIMIT, AND I BOUGHT SOMETHING I CAN'T AFFORD ANYMORE.

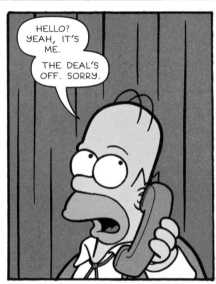

HELLO? YEAH, IT'S ME.

THE DEAL'S OFF. SORRY.

HOMERLAND
E WAY
NO LEFT TURN
BAD NEWS, EVERYONE, WE'RE BACK TO BEING ICELAND AGAIN.
AWWWWWWW!
TELEPHONE
HONE
KEEP TY EAN
THE END

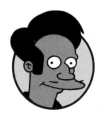

SALUTATIONS TO ALL POTENTIAL KWIK-E CLERKS!
WHAT BETTER WAY TO GET STARTED IN THE COOKIE-CUTTER,
CONVENIENCE STORE TRADE THAN BY BUILDING YOUR VERY OWN
KWIK-E-MART FROM THE GROUND UP THROUGH THE

BUSY HANDS PAPERCRAFT PROJECT!

YOU, TOO, CAN JOIN THE FEW, THE BRAVE, THE SLEEP-DEPRIVED AND DISCOVER
THE ESSENTIALS OF DISPENSING NONESSENTIAL SNACKS AND BRIC-A-BRAC AT
IMMENSELY INFLATED PRICES. FIND YOUR LIFE'S PURPOSE IN REPURPOSABLE
RETAIL! WE'LL MAKE YOU A SQUISHEE™, YOU CAN'T REFUSE!

WHAT YOU WILL NEED:
- Scissors, adhesive tape, and a straight edge (such as a ruler).
- An ability to fold along straight lines.
- An additional "mint condition" copy of this book secured elsewhere!

1. Cut out figures and bases.
2. Cut along the dotted line at the base of each figure and also the center
   of each curved base. (Be careful not to cut too far!)
3. Connect base to figure as shown (Fig. 1).
4. Before cutting out the shapes, use a ruler and a slightly rounded metal tool
   (like the edge of a key) to first score, and then fold lightly along all the interior
   lines (this will make final folds much easier).
5. Cut along the exterior shape. Make sure to cut all the way to where the walls,
   the roof, and the flap lines meet (Fig. 2).

Fig. 1

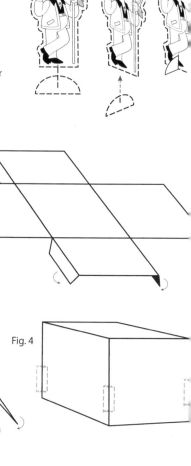

Fig. 2

6. Form building by folding walls
   into place (Fig. 3) and secure all
   tabs to the interior of the
   building with tape (Fig. 4).

Fig. 3

Fig. 4

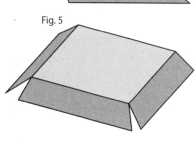

Fig. 5

7. Cut and fold awning shape as shown (Fig. 5),
   and secure with tape. Then, place on top
   of building and secure with looped tape
   between the roof and awning (Fig. 6).
   For added strength, you can run a small piece
   of tape along the back edge of the awning
   shape and the back wall of the building (Fig. 7).

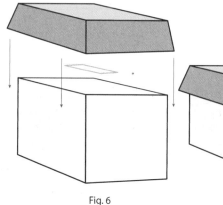

Fig. 6

Fig. 7